DISCOVERING
the Cathars

This book was printed by LoireOffset Titoulet, in Saint-Étienne (42).
The photoengraving is by Photogravure d'Aquitaine and Labogravure, in Bordeaux (33).
ISBN: 978-2-81770-304-6
Éditeur: 01.02.05.13

Discovering
the Cathars

Lucien Bély

Photographs by Jacques Jolfre

Notes and photo captions by Raymond Sicard

Translation by Angela Caldwell

The secret of the Cathars

The Cathar religion has kept its secrets. Ordinary believers were given access to only part of the theology and the "Perfects" i.e. the Cathar clergy, protected it carefully. All that is known about them is what they admitted to the Inquisition when questioned and what has been written about them by polemicists in their attempts to convince or destroy them. Fragments of one of the only Cathar treatises has been passed on in the work by Durand d'Osca (or Huesca), *Liber contra manicheos*, in which the author did his best to refute the religion. "It is the Devil who has created the sons of this century. They were born of the flesh of Sin..." Moreover, it is probable that the Cathar faith was not a unified religion and that trends, or even rivalries, had led to significant differences of opinion and beliefs, even though the so-called "Albigensian" church claimed a degree of unity. The "Pure" (probably the Greek origin of the word "Cathars") may have been found throughout much of Europe but they were to be found in largest numbers in Occitania, the region that later became known as the province of Languedoc.

The uncertainty that surrounds the Cathars and their religion has left great scope for the imagination and nothing seems to lie outside the realms of possibility. Passions have been aroused and have clung onto this phenomenon from the past. References to Catharism have nourished anticlericalism, highlighting the repression implemented by the Roman Catholic Church and the setting up of the Inquisition. The crusade against the Albigensians has also been taken as an argument to show the rigours of the "French conquest" of Occitania. Yet many other treatises have been given prominence to honour a Cathar philosophy which remains ill-defined. In 1940, philosopher Simone Weil saw Catharism as "a pythagorism or a Christian form of platonism" and she wrote, "The Manichaeans have something more than can be found in the days of Ancient Greece and Rome, or at least that part of it known to us. Their beliefs contain a few splendid concepts such as the idea of God descending among Man and the idea of the spirit being ripped apart and dispersed among matter. What makes Catharism a form of miracle, however, is the fact that it was a religion and not simply a philosophy" (letter to Déodat Roché, 23rd January 1940).

Georges Duby has shown that, setting aside partisan fervour, the destiny that befell Catharism touches our conscience from two points of view – firstly, it calls on our idea of tolerance and, secondly, it arouses feelings of nationalism. Why should this "sect", which was tolerated in its early days, have been persecuted and, finally, eradicated? It is difficult for us today to accept that men could have been killed for their religious faith or their ideas in order to impose a single religion and a conformity of ideas for all. Had the Cathars committed acts which justified their being burnt at the stake? And why, in the name of the crusade, i.e. in the name of a Christian ideal, was the South of France subjected to a fearsome military campaign which resulted in the region's barons being dispossessed of their lands? René Nelli went so far as to suggest that the result was the disappearance of an entire civilisation.

Montségur:
castel and village seen from a plane.

Roquefixade
conquering the clouds.

Arques

The crusaders' arrival.
This square keep with its four turrets dates from a period after the crusade against the Cathars. Simon de Montfort gave his companion-in-arms, Pierre de Voisins, command of the fortress and it was de Voisins'descendants who built this masterpiece of military architecture.

Carcassonne

The conflict engendered by Catharism affected the mighty town that was eventually given to the King of France. He made is an essential part of the kingdom's defences in the south. The double walls, which stretch over a distance of 3 kilometres, and the countless towers reflect ongoing changes in the design of fortifications.

Fontfroide

Mediaeval monks such as the Benedictines in Fontfroide built their abbeys in remote places. In the 12th century, they became part of the Cistercian order. As the abbeys gained wealth and erected fortifications thanks to the generosity of Christian believers, the buildings became larger and their austere beauty made them very impressive. The Cathars often reproached the Roman Catholic Church for its displays of wealth and power. Today's travellers, on the other hand, are unfailingly stunned by the breathtakingly beautiful buildings that serve as a reminder of a great era in European architecture (photo by Pascal Moulin).

The temptation of dualism

Because the Cathars recognised that the world was governed by two principles, they were described as "Manichaeans" and, consequently, as dualists. It has to be said from the outset that beliefs such as these already existed in the Middle East. Far back in time, between 1,250 and 500 B.C., a legendary figure named Zoroaster or Zarathustra had created Zoroastrianism or the Mazdean doctrine which recognised two principles in the world, Good or *Ormazd* and Evil or *Ahriman*, locked in perpetual conflict. The religion spread throughout what we now know as Iran but it also had enormous influence on the Jewish prophets and on Greeks such as Pythagorus. Then, in the 3rd Century A. D, Babylon went through the age of Manes or Mani. Manichaeism also stated that there were two principles, Good and Evil, Light and Darkness, God and Matter. During that same period, a sect was founded by Paul of Samsat. It centred on Armenia where the Paulicians, although not Manichaeists, rejected the Old Testament and the Eucharist. Byzantium put an end to the sect in the 9th Century and the Paulicians were deported to the Balkans, a region where there was a major struggle for influence between Rome and Byzantium. Between the two came the Bogomil faith, said to have been named after a religious leader, since Bogomil meant "Friend of God" in the Slav language. As the religion spread among the Bulgarians, the Bogomils were also known as Bulgarians and, by linguistic deformation, as "Buggers". Two authors, Cosmas and Euthime Zigabène, wanted to refute this belief and it is through them that we have acquired knowledge of the Bogomils. Those in the church in Dragovitsa in Thrace (also known as Dragovitia) were radicals who believed that the terrestrial world was the work of the Devil. They rejected the Old Testament and all forms of sacrament since it necessarily included matter created by the Devil. They did not respect the Cross and they led ascetic lives, abstaining from any sexual act and refusing to eat meat. Others, especially in Bulgaria, were more moderate. Like the Manichaeists, they differentiated between the Chosen Few and the ordinary believers. A ceremony involving the laying-on of hands enabled a believer to become one of the Chosen Few. Dualism spread through Italy, where the Cathars were also described as Patarins, and also became widespread elsewhere in the Christian world. In 1250, a former high-ranking Cathar named Rainier Sacconi, having become an Inquisitor in Lombardy, indicated that there were five Cathar churches in France (Toulouse, Albi, Carcassonne, Agen and the North of France), six in Italy (Desenzano, Concorezzo, Bagnolo, Vicenza, Florence and the Spoleto Valley) and six in the Middle East (Dragovitia, Bulgaria, Philadelphia, Slavonia, and two in Constantinople, one of them Greek and the other Latin). In the mid 13th Century, by which time the Church of Rome had already instigated an armed struggle against the Cathars in the Western world, the churches seemed to have acquired close ties with each other, like a vast, pan-European, spiritual movement alhough it stretched out mainly along the shores of the Mediterranean.

Many questions have been posed as to the nature and origins of this faith. Was Catharism in the Western world no more than a resurgence and extension of very ancient religions from very distant lands? Was this the birth of a new Church that posed a threat to the Christian Church in both Rome and Byzantium? Or was it merely a strange, original, new form of Christianity, perhaps even a return to original Christianity?

Just one more heresy?

In the eyes of the Church, these religious doctrines were heresies and, as such, they had to be fought with every means at its disposal. The Papacy paid little heed to the origin of the beliefs and practices. As soon as they appeared to become incompatible with essential dogma, they had to be eradicated. Catharism, though, was not the only mediaeval heresy to be condemned by the Church authorities and the Cathars

were not the only people to be burnt at the stake. Many of the unusual features of this religious movement were to be found in other spiritual movements that had no dualist bases e.g. the refusal to baptise children, virulent criticism of the clergy, refusal to believe in the real presence of Christ in the Eucharist, the refusal to eat meat or bow before the Cross which was the scene of Christ's suffering, etc.

Two historical theses confronted each other, especially with regard to the origins of Catharism. On one hand, there were those who saw oriental influence in all heresies. They had certain points in common despite the fact that they originated in places far away from each other and, if brought together, the scattered elements corresponded to the beliefs that had become prevalent in Bulgaria. A 20th-century scholar, Father Dondaine, followed others in supporting this hypothesis. Jean Duvernoy, a historian specialising in Catharism, and Jacques Le Goff, a well-known mediaeval scholar, both acknowledge the possibility of links with the Balkans. One of the proofs of this link is the Council said to have taken place in Saint-Félix-Lauragais in 1167 at which, as we shall see, "Pope" Nicetas, an envoy from Constantinople, is thought to have been present.

Other historians such as Raffaelo Morghen, on the other hand, have refuted any idea of the heresies' having their origins in the Middle East. They are said to have grown up on the spot, without any real theological coherence, and to have been based on moral and social factors. The heresies are said to have attracted mainly the illiterate who were hungry for a more rigourous morality and hostile to the wealthy clergy with their lavish lifestyles. This interpretation bears similarities to the Marxist viewpoint put forward initially by Engels. Marxists saw these heretical movements as a form of social uprising against an established order symbolised and embodied by the Church which left little or no room for individualism.

Termes: the rallying point.
This cross-shaped window is in the castle chapel.

St. Mary's Chapel, Peyrepertuse.
The chapel dates from before 1115 and is a Romanesque building.
The apse has semi-circular barrel vaulting. The altar has been uncovered.

opposite:
Carcassonne. The hoardings, machicolations, drawbridge
and gateway on the count's castle.

Termes Castle.

Termes Castle, or the impossible task of withstanding the onslaught of the crusaders. The de Termes family was closely involved in the Cathar movement. Benoît de Termes was appointed Bishop of the Razès area in 1226 when the "heretical" hierarchy opposed the Roman Catholic Church.

Peyrepertuse.

The lower castle known as the "Old Keep".

-----

opposite:

Peyrepertuse.

This spur of rock in the Upper Corbières region stood guard over the border separating the kingdoms of France and Aragon.

Two interpretations

There are, then, two opposing interpretations. One is primarily religious in nature, following ideas and dogmas through time and space, monitoring developments in ritualistic practices and the organisation of the churches. Catharism is seen, in this case, as part of a long line of dualist philosophies rooted in the East and dating far back in time. The official Churches became aware of these strange tendencies in the 11th and 12th Centuries and tried to control them or, later, from the 13th Century onwards, to eradicate them altogether. The other interpretation minimises the independence of the religious aspect. It simply observes that dogma did exist but was always present, being a natural but concealed part of life which came to the fore as a result of certain political, economic or social situations.

In an attempt to explain the spontaneous creation of Catharism, there are those who saw it as an extension of Christian gnosticism, and others who saw it as perhaps having connections with Jewish spirituality. The exchange of manuscripts is said to explain certain similarities or coincidences at a time when the Jewish religion was marked by the esoterics of the Cabbala, a concept which was born in Languedoc, in towns such as Lunel and Narbonne, at the end of the 12th Century. It should, though, be said that the Cathars were also highly suspicious of the Jews for it was they who had brought the Old Testament.

Mediaeval christianity shaken to the core

Catharism has often been understood and imagined outside its historical context i.e. the Christianity of the Middle Ages, and has been seen cloaked in the colours of a modernity that it did not possess. Heresies, including Catharism, prospered in the 11th and 12th Centuries at a time when the reforms instigated by Pope Gregory VII (1020-1085) were becoming more generally accepted. The Pope and cardinals had themselves attacked the simony of the priesthood, i.e. the willingess on the part of priests to give sacraments in exchange for financial reward. Simony, though, was difficult to define (any gift to the Church could look like simony) and the criticism fuelled the popular mistrust of ecclesiastics. This was all the more true inasmuch as a bishop accused of simony was not entitled to ordain a priest and he, in turn, could not give the sacraments to a congregation. This led to systematic denigration of priests and mistrust as regards the sacraments administered by them such as the Eucharist or baptism. Added to this, there was a refusal to worship an object rather than God. Pictures and other representations of Christ were open to condemnation and churches themselves were gradually seen as useless. Many of these temptations corresponded to an extreme view of the Christian faith. A large number of religious orders did not eat meat and the celibacy of the priesthood could be seen as a refusal of a carnal act that was considered as a sin. Those who were sentenced as heretics may have been carried away by the very principles that had been defended during the Gregorian reform and, by doing so, they had placed themselves outside the realm of Christian rules. Yet the men described as heretics were not so very far removed from the hermits and preachers who were proclaiming the need for a return to a purer form of faith and a purer lifestyle. This was why they cut themselves off from the usual world, but it is perhaps not unreasonable to suggest that the crusaders who took up the Cross in order to fight also cut themselves off from their everyday environment. Heretics, then, were adventurers as well as religious and social dissidents and there is often a very fine line between a saint and a heretic. Should this also be seen as a revolt against the wealth and power of local noblemen or prelates? Was it a form of social struggle? Care is required here. Some of the heretics were peasants, but not all of them. They broke away from the sin that was present in the world of the peasant but it was the same sin that could be found among clerks and princes and they broke away from it in order to improve the world they were leaving behind, not in order to destroy it.

What was the social background of the Cathars, in particular the Perfects in Languedoc? There are those who emphasise the fact that Catharism prospered in the Lauragais area where the population was largely illiterate and in working-class areas whereas in Toulouse, for example, the town of Counts and officers, troubadours and merchants, it had very little effect. If this is so, Catharism would be a popular revolt against a dominant religion and social structure, in short an uprising of the poorest members of society. Other historians show that, early in the 13th Century, a new generation of Cathars appeared on the scene, this time recruited from among the nobility, and that it was this change which worried Rome. The papacy could see the social elite, the "executives" of society as a whole, moving away from the Roman Catholic Church, taking with them their vassals and peasants.

St. George's Chapel, Peyrepertuse.

This is the chapel in the "new" keep that was built during the reign of St. Louis. It was dedicated to St. Georges (Sant-Jordi in Occitan). All that remains of the church is the West gable.

Béziers.

The interior of the cathedral which was rebuilt after having been set on fire during the siege of the town (photo by Pascal Moulin).

opposite:

Béziers.

St. Nazaire's Cathedral is shrouded in memories of the Albigensian Crusade (photo by Pascal Moulin).

René Nelli, who has written a large number of books on Catharism and the troubadours, nevertheless insisted on all the factors that separated Catharism and the feudal system or mediaeval society. Like everything in life, the social hierarchy could only be a creation of the Devil; it was not a reflection of the will of God. And only the will of God was worthy of respect. Birth, i.e. Nature, sperm and blood, the factor that created social distinctions, was in no way sacred since it was a satanic illusion. There was no reason why justice should be meted out by noblemen and, in Montségur, the Cathar bishops insisted that all quarrels be submitted to them for arbitration. Oaths, a fundamental aspect of feudal society forming a link between the vassal and the sovereign that was based on honour, were also rejected by the Cathars – quite simply, Perfects did not lie. And warfare, the main activity of knights and the justification for the privileges enjoyed by them, was also condemned. This was indeed a return to evangelical doctrine and it was also the official doctrine of the Roman Catholic Church. In Catharism, though, it was taken to extremes, to its utmost limits, to breaking point.
One thing that is sure is that the Cathars had followers among the nobility and, in the end, in order to describe these believers who have disappeared without trace and have left very little documentary evidence of their existence, men now turn quite naturally to the impregnable citadels to which the mediaeval barons invited these God-fearing fervents. Although many of these fortresses have undergone alterations since the end of the heresy, the geographical locations and the landscapes give some hint of the extravagance of the threat posed to Rome and Paris, indeed to the entire world. Moreover, once the noblemen of Southern France had engaged in the struggle against the crusaders or the monarch, they were forced to seek the backing of the Cathars even though they did not necessarily share their views and, in some cases, had already persecuted them. Yet they needed them in order to mobilise people in the face of the threat posed by the army from the North.

Albi.
St. Cecilia's Cathedral resembles a fortress.
It was built after the Albigensian Crusade as protection against any other heretical movements in the future (photo by Jeanne Duprat).

More trivial reasons have been put forward to explain the advance of Catharism. It is said that the nobility was pleased to see the Cathars attack a Church that possessed enormous wealth, wealth that was coveted by these very noblemen. The tolerance shown towards the Jews in Southern France has also been looked at carefully. Did the ecclesiastical authorities see this as a threat? It is said that Jews accompanied the Viscount of Béziers when he fled his town in the face of the crusaders'advance. Yet was it not also true that the Cathars, by ignoring the Old Testament, denied the Jewish legacy that was part of the Christian faith? Historians have also emphasised that latent conflicts opposed the Church and southern French princes who discreetly supported their subjects when they did not pay their taxes to the Church, in particular the tithes.
Nowadays, the phenomenon of the Cathars is associated with Occitania, i.e. with a linguistic region. It cannot, however, be seen without its political dimension. The kingdom of France had let large principalities grow and develop, and the spread of their influence overshadowed the modest Capetian monarch tied to his lands in the Paris Basin. The Count of Toulouse was one of the princes who had gained almost total independence from his theoretical sovereign. Raimond, Abbot of Saint-Gilles-du-Gard, the Count's younger son, had succeeded in imposing his authority in the 11th Century over an area that stretched from Provence to Gascony. In the 12th Century, Raimond V had a position tantamount to that of a sovereign prince, and, moreover, a prince with considerable influence in the Western world. Toulouse was a powerful, densely-populated town and the Count's Court was brilliant and lavish.
Yet the Count had to withstand pressure from his neighbours, in particular the Trencavels, the powerful family that controlled Carcassonne, Albi and Béziers. The Trencavels were vassals of the Count of Barcelona who was also the King of Aragon, with influence stretching right along the Pyrenees. Given that the Spanish princes were then moving to recapture the Iberian Peninsula from the Saracen, what action might they take to the North of the mountain range? Then there were the Counts of Foix. In this family, many of the women were Cathar "Perfects". Yet Catharism had not spread throughout all the lands belonging to these noblemen. It was commonest in a geographical area stretching from Toulouse in the West to Carcassonne in the East, and from the outcrops of the Pyrenees in the South to the Mon-

tagne Noire in the North. Jean Duvernoy describes it as an "epicentre" and emphasises that the heresy spread all the more easily in areas where political and religious control was weakest, i.e. the western part of the Count of Toulouse' lands to which he paid very little heed.

After the crusade against the Albigensians, the political situation was thrown into total upheaval. The Count of Toulouse acknowledged the sovereignty of the King of France who already had strong control over the South of his country even before he annexed it, making it an integral part of his kingdom. The independence of the principalities was no more than a memory and national identity began to grow and strengthen. Meanwhile, the King of France kept a particularly watchful eye on this border area because it was vital for the kingdom of France, in the face of threats from the princes in the Iberian Peninsula.

Foix.

The women of the family all became Perfects.

The Counts of Foix protected the Cathars and the family's womenfolk became Perfects. Yet the county of Foix submitted to royal authority and the Counts remained influential princes until the end of the Middle Ages.

Usson.

Little remains of the old castle except these impressive ruins and the section of keep jutting up from their midst.

opposite:

Peyrepertuse: a challenge to Nature.

The lower wall and the spur of rock at the eastern end. To the right are the apartments with their "mod. cons." (sinks, latrines and postern gate).

Padern.

The castle was occupied during the crusade then recaptured by its dispossessed noblemen.

-----

above:

Miglose: the Lords of the Mountains.

The Lord of Miglos was a Cathar and this isolated, ruined castle is a fine example of the destiny of families such as his who were drawn to a new religion that eventually caused their downfall.

Carcassonne.

The Count's Castle.

Cathar metaphysics and morality

The underlying concept in Catharism was the problem of Evil. Christian faith insisted on this factor and the Cathars took it to its logical, but extreme, conclusion. Since God is perfect and is the Creator of everything, how could He have created Evil in the form of misfortune, pain, and sin? There had to be another explanation. In the dualism described by historians as moderate or mitigated, it was Lucifer, a fallen angel, who created Evil. For absolute dualists, there is a radical distinction between Good and Evil, making material reality the creation of the Devil. Christ could not have come down to earth as a man since He would then have been participating in this reality. His incarnation was nothing but an illusion. He cannot be present in the Eucharist since the wafer is matter and cannot therefore be transformed into God. Procreation perpetuates the visible world and is therefore condemned. Hence the refusal to allow Perfects to marry. A sacrament cannot cover an action seen as detrimental to spiritual life. Catharism is, then, marked by radical pessimism. "There results from this, as far as the Albigensian religion is concerned, a deeper, radical and insurmountable pessimism that is expressed in the well-known claim that the Last Judgement has already occurred and that the guilty are already in Hell, i.e. to be more precise on earth. Mankind is made up of the damned for whom there is nothing but suffering, misfortune, death and imprisonment; they are enclosed in the matter that perpetuates and produces the sexual instinct through which the chain of Evil is passed on from one being to another. Sexuality is therefore seen as a diabolical trap, a horrible, repugnant snare that closes in on all living reality" (R. Manselli).

The mediaeval scholar, Francis Rapp, has shown that Christianity was seeking unity at any cost since it felt threatened by other religions on its borders and by returns to paganism and ancient myths within its own frontiers. In the name of this essential unity, the Church denounced any criticism of its dogmas. The real presence of Christ in the Eucharist and the incarnation of the Son of God as man formed the very bases of the Christian religion. Anybody shaking these pillars of faith would overturn the entire structure, i.e. the ecclesiastical institution as well as the spiritual and moral coherence offered to the world by Christianity. Catharism itself had developed in the western world, especially in Languedoc. "The internal evolution of Catharism in the western

world undoubtedly played a part in its downfall. By the end of the 12th Century, it had adopted the radical dualism professed by the Thracian Church in Dragowitsa. From then on, it could no longer describe itself as an authentic form of Christianity. Its preaching, which had been able to take advantage of its superficial resemblance with the Gospels as long as its own dogmas had remained vague, began to lack support once the huge gap that separated its own theology from that of Christianity had become apparent. Newcomers were fewer in number and they could not longer fill the breaches caused by executions" (F. Rapp). The crucial moment for a Cathar believer was the *consolamentum* which ensured his or her eternal salvation. This was the only hope in the pessimistic vision of creation. This ritual, or sacrament, was administered by Perfects when a believer was on the point of death but only if he was still conscious and could recite a prayer. The Cathars had energetically refused the idea of Catholic baptism because the baby was not yet conscious of his actions, so, taking this concept to its logical conclusion, a believer could no longer receive the *consolamentum* if he was no longer able to speak. This led to the expedient of the *conveNentia* or *convenensa*. The believer could receive the *consolamentum* even if he was unable to speak and this was particularly useful as the Perfects found it more and more difficult to reach the sick. The importance placed on the *consolamentum* may have been the reason for the instigation of the *endura*, suicide by starvation, a practice about which historians have never been able to agree. If the believer survived, there was a risk that he might commit sins and so lose the benefit of the sacrament. In order to avoid this risk, it is said that a person having been given the *consolamentum* then sought to die by refusing to eat. This form of suicide is also said to have been reflected in the courage shown by the believers when they were taken to be burnt at the stake. Some historians consider the *endura* as an off-shoot of a Catharism in decline while others believe that the practice existed in the spiritual movement from its inception. As the *consolamentum* was the means to salvation, the Roman

-----

Carcassonne.

The Guardian of Southern France.

The walled town summarises all that was most spectacular in military architecture. The Trencavels'castle was on the West side of the town.

Catholic sacraments no longer served any purpose. In particular, confession and penitence were useless and this was another means of escaping the influence of priests who used these practices to gain closer access to parishioners' souls.
The *consolamentum* also enabled believers to become Perfects or, as the Cathars called them, Good Men or Friends of God. After the ceremony, a Perfect had to cease committing sins. From then on, he or she could administer the *consolamentum* to believers on their death beds. It no doubt required a long period of initiation before a believer earned the right to give others the *consolamentum*. The Cathars were required to show respect for the Perfects by "adoring" them i.e. by bowing or genuflecting three times to them. In return, the Perfects blessed those who adored them. This practice was also known as the *melhorament*. It is, then, reasonable to assume that the Perfects were easily recognisable. Until 1230, they had long hair and beards, dressed in black and wore a round hat but persecution doubtless led them to abandon these distinctive signs.
The Cathar vision of salvation extended to belief in metempsychosis. People who had not received the *consolamentum* believed that their soul would wander from one being to another and that they could be born again as an animal. Because of this, believers were forbidden to kill any living creature since it could contain a human soul. One of the Perfects was a horse in a former life. One day, passing the spot where he had lost a shoe when he had been a horse, he remembered the incident and told his companion about it. They began looking for the horse shoe and found it.
A man could be reincarnated as a woman and this may have been a factor in the equality of the sexes in the Cathar religion. Even if women were the Devil's favourite victim, they were nevertheless entitled to become Perfects. In this case, they were considered to be on an equal footing with their male counterparts and could preach sermons. This was very appropriate in a world where troubadours exalted the place of women and love in their poetry.

Heresy revealed

It was in the 12th Century that the ecclesiastical authorities became aware of the threat hanging over Languedoc, but the same threat also existed elsewhere. In 1143, the Provost of the Premonstratensians in Steinfeld in the Rhineland wrote to Bernard of Clairvaux (the future St. Bernard) who, with the Cistercian monks, had reformed the Benedictine Order. Heretics had been discovered and two of them had entered a debate during a meeting of clerks and laity. They had maintained their views and had been burnt at the stake by an "over-zealous population"! Those who had bowed to pressure, admitted that the heresy had existed since the days of the Apostles and that the heretics constituted "a multitude of people over the whole face of the earth".
St. Bernard soon realised the extent of the movement. He began to worry about the actions of a former Benedictine monk, Henri, and in 1145 decided to travel to the South of France. There he realised that the climate was favourable to heretical beliefs and that heresy was rife, even among the nobility. Likewise, the climate and situation helped the cause of people such as this disturbing monk. In Verfeil, Bernard is said to have accused the nobility of turning a blind eye to the heretics, and the noblemen swept out of the church followed by the ordinary people. The terrible man of God continued to harangue them outside the church but the noblemen then hammered on the doors to drown out his voice. Bernard cursed the town with a pun, "Verfeil ("verte feuille" meaning "green leaf"), may God cause you to wither!" It was Bernard's companions, the Cistercians of the Order of Cîteaux, who led the first offensives against the Cathars, at a time when other monastic Orders and parish priests showed little hostility towards them. St. Bernard kept an eye on the heretics in Southern France while preaching the crusade against the Infidel who had captured Jerusalem.
It was even difficult to name the heretics. They were sometimes known as "Aryans" after the great heresy dating back to the beginnings of the Christian Era, and sometimes called "weavers" or "Manichaeans". They described themselves as "Good Christians" and their Perfects as Good Men or Good Women. They were also traditionally known as Albigensians although, paradoxically, the town of Albi was not one of the main centres of Catharism.
Gradually, details emerged that gave a clearer picture of these different people. They ate no meat, often knelt down, refused Communion, did not bow to the Cross or images of Christ, and refused to accept the authority of the Old Testament.

The powerlessness of the Cistercians

Councils passed sentence on the heretics and their protectors but the dialogue remained open. In 1165, a council or meeting took place in Lombers, attended by prelates and representatives of what must be called a "sect". The Cathars built their entire defence on the letter of the scriptures. And the Good Men were setting up a veritable organisation. A Pope, or "papas" is said to have come from the Cathar church in Constantinople in 1167 to chair a council held in Saint-Félix de Caraman (now known as Saint-Félix de Lauragais). A document, which is the subject of some controversy, tells how bishops were chosen for Lombardy, Northern France, Albi, Toulouse, Carcassonne and Agen and how limits were suggested for a Cathar church that was beginning to look like a counter-Church, with its own hierarchy. The largest number of bishops was said to have been appointed for Languedoc, a sign perhaps that the heresy had found more fertile ground and a higher number of followers there than elsewhere. Raoul Manselli, like Father Dondaine, placed enormous importance on this event. It marked the unification of the Cathar church from southern France to Lombardy, and was a U-turn in that it revealed a radical form of dualism and an affirmation of a more polemic doctrine. This was the real birth of the Albigensian church.
In 1177, the Count of Toulouse sent a letter to the Chapter General of the Order of Cîteaux, denouncing the spread of the heresy. "... Those in charge of church affairs stink of heresy. The old, and once venerable, places in the churches are untended or remain in ruins. Christenings have been refused, the Eucharist has been abominated, and penitence seen as totally unimportant. The creation of mankind and the resurrection of the body are rejected as untrue. All the church sacraments are cancelled and, even more terrible than this, two principles have been introduced." This letter

-----

Quéribus, facing northwards.
Three outer walls protect the huge keep which was the main element in the system of defence from the outset. Quéribus withstood attack by the barons from Northern France when Chabert de Barbeira was officer-in-command but, in 1471, it fell to the army of Aragon without a struggle.

was doubtless a piece of political manoeuvring but it shows, nevertheless, that the heresy had become vitally important in Europe.

A group of Cistercians came to the Toulouse area on a mission and held a debate, in Toulouse itself, with two of the leading heretics of the day, Bernard Raimond and Raimond de Baimiac, who were protected by safe conducts. The Cathars complained of the treatment they had suffered at the hands of the Count of Toulouse who had banished them from his lands. They described their profession of faith, without proclaiming anything untoward, and people attending the debate protested, saying that the men believed in two gods, one of them good and the other one evil. What was more, they contested the presence of Christ during a consecration ceremony carried out by an unworthy priest and condemned conjugal duties. The Catholic priests could do little more than repeat to the two Cathars that they had been excommunicated. The Church, however, did not go so far as to introduce capital punishment, restricting itself to the imposition of acts of penitence such as pilgrimages. These were days of glory for the Order of Cîteaux – St. Bernard had just been canonised. Cardinal Henri de Marcy, former Abbot of Clairvaux, managed to raise a small army and he captured the two Cathars who had gone to Toulouse. They acknowledged their heresy and abjured. They then became canons of the Roman Catholic Church, one in St. Sernin's and the other at the Church of St. Stephen (Saint-Etienne) in Toulouse. This was a success for the Roman Catholic Church and an honourable way out for the Cathar leaders.

Dangers abound

Catharism enjoyed a golden age in the early years of the 13th Century. Ladies of high birth such as Esclarmonde of Foix, sister of the Count of Foix, became Perfects. This time, heresy spread through families that were almost considered as sovereigns, proof that it was no longer an underground movement. Texts use the simple term "heretics" to describe those who had received the *consolamentum*. The conversions of members of the nobility showed that the social elite was attracted to the new religion. The pessimistic outlook, moral rigour and ideal of renunciation were particularly attractive to souls in search of the absolute. This also meant that the Roman Catholic message was no longer sufficient for them. The Roman Catholic Church found itself in danger for the Perfects who were of noble extraction were likely to have followers, especially as knowledge and the art of public speaking were widespread among the upper social classes and these were converts with great talent for persuading others to join them in their new beliefs. They could draw with them, in the heretic movement, men and women of lower ranks in the highly-structured social order. There was, too, a decline in moral values. The troubadours had sung the praises of a love that was often idealised, a love of the noble lady, and their feelings had produced reactions in the Southern French civilisation. Thereafter, noble ladies were no longer attracted by flirting; instead, they were drawn to a doctrine of solitude and austerity. The earliest Cathars may have come from the illiterate classes but, by the early 13th Century, the movement had spread throughout the social fabric. The King of Aragon travelled to Carcassonne (a town over which he had sovereign rights) in 1204 to renew his condemnation of the heretics, but he took no real action against them. Meanwhile, tension was mounting.

The Cistercians were busy in Languedoc. One of the monks from the Cistercian Fontfroide Abbey, Pierre de Castelnau, was a papal legate i.e. he had wide-ranging powers and

opposite:

A flight of steps in Quéribus...

The steps to the keep. Visitors now have to use their imagination if they want to have some idea of what everyday life was like in these impregnable fortresses.

-----

above:

Aguilar Castle.

The West side, still protected by an outer wall and several towers.

-----

left:

Dominic's House in Fanjeaux.

It is difficult to imagine, as you stroll through the quiet streets of Fanjeaux, that this was once a hotbed of Catharism but in those days it was a town, with its own noblemen and its Perfects' Houses. St Dominic took up residence here and turned Fanjeaux into the centre of his quest to reconquer lost souls.

was the Pope's personal representative. He began to attack Count Raimond VI of Toulouse. By 1206, the Cistercians had succeeded in imposing one of their number, a former troubadour named Foulque de Marseille, as Bishop of Toulouse. He was one of the most enthusiastic detractors of the Cathar religion. And the Abbot General of Cîteaux, Arnaud Amaury, was appointed legate. Yet all these monks were powerless in the face of the vitality of the Cathar religion.

Dominic

It was at this point that Dominic arrived in Languedoc. He was following Diego, Bishop of Osma in Spain and was subprior to the chapter of the cathedral in Osma. Diego and Dominic met the papal legates and the Cistercians, all of whom had failed in their conversion attempts. The two Spaniards criticised their lavish lifestyles and advised them to go preaching on foot, show steadfastness, and make a display of their poverty. In short, they were to beat the Cathars at their own game. Dominic had spent a whole night talking to the inn-keeper where he had stayed in Toulouse. The man was a Cathar and the future saint realised just how far the heresy had spread and how mediocre were the methods used to stamp it out. A debate was held in Montréal. The Roman Catholic Church was represented by Diego, Dominic, Pierre de Castelnau and his colleague, Raoul; the Cathars included Arnaud Hot, Benoît de Termes, Pons Jourda and Guilhabert de Castres. The chronicler of the event recounted how each of the sides remitted their writings to arbitrators, in this instance two noblemen and two wealthy merchants. The discussion is said to have lasted a fortnight. At this point, legend takes over. "One of our men, named Dominic, a man steeped in saintliness who had been the companion of the Bishop of Osma, wrote down the quotations that he had used during the debate. He gave the piece of paper to one of the heretics so that he could review the man's objections. During the night, the heretics gathered round the fire in a house. The one to whom the man of God had given the sheet of paper handed it round his companions. They then suggested that the paper should be thrown into the fire. If the paper burned, their beliefs (i.e. their misbeliefs) would be proved to be true. If, on the other hand, it did not burn, they would confess the truth of the credo put forward by our preachers." The paper withstood the flames three times. However, the theological debate held in Montréal, even if it did not lead to any obvious results, was a victory for the Cathar Church which was able to discuss matters with the representatives of the official Church on an equal footing. Diego of Osma left Languedoc but his follower, Dominic, remained behind. At the end of 1206, Dominic founded a convent for a dozen converted heretic women in Prouille, downhill from Fanjeaux, a major centre of the Cathar faith. The women were given an income by the Bishop of Narbonne and Dominic was careful not to change the lifestyle they had known when they were Perfects. This was one way of facilitating conversions and making sure that the nobility, especially those faced with financial difficulties, did not get rid of their daughters by giving them to the Cathar Church. St. Dominic poses something of a paradox. He was popular. Once he had set up his community of converts in Prouille, he submitted his ideas to Rome where they were accepted and soon "Dominicans" were to be found throughout the world, which proved the fairness of Dominic's teaching and

-----

opposite:
Aguilar Castle.
From this tower,
there is a panoramic view of the surrounding countryside.

below:
Durfort and the Orbieu River.
The owners of the castle formed an influential family and they were drawn to the heresy.
The fortress stands in a landscape created by the waters of the R. Orbieu.

the strength of his example. However, even today, there is still an awkwardness when Dominic's name is mentioned because the first Inquisitors were Dominicans. And those who admire the saint remain perplexed when confronted by the mission entrusted to his followers.

Jean Duvernoy puts the emphasis on St. Dominic's trips to Rome where the Pope is said to have entrusted him with the difficult task of bringing the Cathars back into the fold of the Roman Catholic Church by meeting their aspirations. The poverty of Dominic and his followers was designed to ward off the criticisms of luxury and opulence that were levelled against the prelates. Their intellectual qualities and their skills as preachers ensured that the religious and moral questions posed by the Cathars were fully answered. The Order founded by St. Dominic was recognised in 1216 and the Dominicans were appointed by the Pope to preach the faith as early as 1217; they became known as the Preaching Friars (or Black Friars). The task set by the Pope was clear, "We thank God who has made you preachers, veritable athletes of the True Faith, and we order you to continue to preach, in return for the remission of your sins." The lifestyle of the Dominican communities, who lived in the country rather than in towns, was reminiscent of the lifestyle of the most fervent Cathars in its austerity and rhythm. This made it easier for Perfects to pass from heresy to a Dominican community without any great difficulty.

Another debate was held in Pamiers where Esclarmonde de Foix is said to have voiced an opinion. A monk is said to have declared, peremptorily, "Get back to your distaff, woman!"

Recourse to a crusade

There were many other heresies in the Western world during the mediaeval period and Catharism could be found elsewhere than in Languedoc (or Occitania), including the Rhineland, Lombardy and Northern France. Why, then, was the region that stretches out along the foothills of the Pyrenees between the sea and Gascony considered as the main centre of the Cathar faith? Because this was the setting for the Crusade. The heresy was the opportunity, or the pretext, to launch a crusade in a world where this form of battle in the name of the True Faith was pregnant with meaning. This time, though, the crusaders' enemies were not unknown Moslems and the crusaders were not fighting in distant lands. This was a crusade against men close to them, on land in the very heart of the Western world; in short it was a war between neighbours and brothers. The solution put forward by Rome and Pope Innocent III was a radical one indeed. For many years, meetings and theological debate had been possible, showing that there was at least a determination to maintain a form of dialogue. The murder of the papal legate, Pierre de Castelnau, however, was a political act inasmuch as the Count of Toulouse was involved in it. It also showed that complicity with the "heretics" had reached the highest echelons of society, namely the Count i.e. a prince who was almost a sovereign in his own right. Was there, then, a risk that an entire part of Christianity might escape the control of Rome? The Church decided that it was time for repression, enforced with military violence thanks to the arrival, in huge numbers, of barons from the north of France and, indeed, other parts of Europe. They swept through the whole of Southern France. However, once the knights suspected of complaisance or mere tolerance had been brought to heel, there remained the problem of how to reconquer souls and impress those who were still tempted by heterodox ideas. It was the Inquisition, with its meticulous attention to detail and its infinite patience, that undertook this systematic enquiry and eradicated the Cathar heresy.

The papal legates accused the noblemen of showing too much kindness to the enemies of the Established Church. Count Raimond VI of Toulouse was the first noblemen to be marked out and it was true that he showed great reluctance to persecute the Cathars since there were followers of the heresy among the highest-ranking nobility, and some among his close friends and relations. No doubt, too, he was pleased to be able to make a show of independence, like all the princes of Christendom, in the face of pontifical might. The Count of Toulouse also acted as a go-between for his own vassals and subjects who looked kindly upon the Perfects. In the end, their tolerance was little more than a form of indifference with regard to theological dispute. The representatives of Rome criticised the Count of Toulouse for having on his payroll troops of mercenaries who ransacked churches and monasteries.

The keep in Quéribus.

This superb chamber with its ribbed vaulting proves that the fortresses continued to be used after the Cathars had been brought to their knees. The defensive system was reorganised in Quéribus and accommodation had to be found for the castle governor.

Les Cassès.

This strange statue of Christ in Prayer is said by René Nelli to be "one of the few figurative remains of the Cathar faith".

The murdered legate

The Pope passed sentence. Raimond VI was excommunicated, i.e. was prohibited from taking part in the sacraments, and this released his subjects from any commitment towards him. Relations between the Count and the papal legate, Pierre de Castelnau, were exceedingly strained. One of the Count's equerries, probably without Raimond's authorisation, decided to seek revenge on his master's behalf. He murdered Pierre de Castelnau in Saint-Gilles-du-Gard just as the prelate was preparing to cross the river Rhône (15th January 1208). This was a serious act because a man of God had been murdered by one of the Count's men and because Pierre was the representative of the Pope, one might almost say he was a living image of the Pope. The papacy placed responsibility for the murder on Raimond and acquired a pretext to push things even further. Arnaud Amaury, Abbot of Cîteaux, put pressure on the Pope to launch a crusade. Guilhem de Tudela, author of *La chanson de la croisade albigeoise*, quoted an eyewitness who was an ambassador to Rome and who reported the Pope as having declared, "From the walls of Montpellier to the gates of Bordeaux, every rebel must be slain." When calling the crusade, Pope Innocent III granted the crusaders absolution for past or future sins. He ordered the Abbot of Cîteaux to lead the army to Carcassonne and Toulouse to fight the renegades. He proclaimed that Raimond VI's lands would become the property of anybody who could capture them.

Arnaud Amaury reached Cîteaux and sent his brothers out to announce the Pope's orders. Noblemen from northern France, the Anglo-Norman kingdom and the German Empire took up arms and regrouped in the Rhône Valley. This mobilisation worried the barons of the South. The Count of Toulouse is said to have suggested to his nephew, Raimond-Roger Trencavel, Viscount of Béziers and Carcassonne, that they might set up a defensive alliance but the young man apparently refused. Raimond VI made his peace with the Church on 18th June 1209 and offered to become a crusader. By doing so, he deflected the storm clouds that were gathering on the edges of his lands and sent them off towards the Trencavels' estates. He did public penance and was whipped, in the presence of a huge crowd, on the very spot where Pierre de Castelnau had been assassinated.

"Kill them all..."

Should these acts of horror be seen as madness on the part of "the army's hangers-on", the footsoldiers who accompanied the crusaders? Should the massacres be seen as intimidation tactics such as had already been used by crusaders, among them King Louis VII of France or Emperor Frederick Barberossa? Should we accept the poet's version of this battle of crusaders, "Any castle that resists and any town unwilling to surrender shall be taken by force and all its people put to the sword. Not even newborn babes shall be left alive. This will spread a healthy terror and nobody shall venture to stand up to the Cross of God"? The people of Béziers had sought refuge in the churches and were massacred. Seven thousand of them were said to have been killed in the Church of St. Mary Magdalene alone. In the eyes of people from the South, the real horror lay in the fact that the crusaders made no distinction between Catholics and heretics. Arnaud Amaury is reported to have said, "Kill them all; the Lord will recognise His own!" This statement, reported by Césaire de Heisterbach, would seem to indicate that the crusade was changing. This was no longer a religious matter in which soldiers were undertaking police work in the name of the Church. This was no longer a traditional piece of feudal warfare limited in time and space. This was punishment for an entire population considered as accomplices. For the barons of Southern France, it was a time of immense trial and tribulation when their property lay under threat. For the ordinary people, it was an invasion during which everybody, even a good Roman Catholic, risked his or her life simply because family, friends or neighbours had chosen to follow the Cathars. Yet the army was not large enough to dominate this vast area of land. They could not have achieved their aims without the relative consent of local populations who had doubtless realised that the heretics had confronted the True Faith and had to be punished, even if good Catholics had to suffer at the same time.

Then came the Siege of Carcassonne. The young Trencavel saw the army of crusaders arrive beneath the walls of his town and he prepared the defence of a citadel that had once withstood attack by Charlemagne himself. The besiegers succeeded in capturing the path that ran down to the river Aude, after a bloody battle, and very soon the population inside the walls was decimated by thirst and epidemics in the torrid heat of summer. King Peter II of Ara-

Fontfroide.
From left to right, this photograph shows the church, cloisters and, finally, the 18th-century courtyard.
Monastic life had given rise to a style of architecture that was majestic for its very simplicity.

THE SACKING OF BÉZIERS

The army of crusaders left Lyons on 24th June 1209 under the leadership of the Abbot of Cîteaux and accompanied by a large number of bishops. The size of the army should not be exaggerated. There were, perhaps, 6000 knights with their usual followers. The *Chanson* contains the names of the most illustrious crusaders, among them the Duke of Burgundy, the Count of Nevers, the Count of Saint-Pol, the Count of Auxerre, the Count of Geneva, and Pierre-Bermond, Lord of Anduze and Sauve. Certain noblemen from the South of France also took up arms in answer to the bishops' call, including Count Gui of Auvergne, the Viscount de Turenne and Bertrand de Cardaillac. The crusaders spread terror from the very start. The army from the north headed for Béziers from which the Viscount had fled in order to fall back on Carcassonne. The Bishop of Béziers tried to convince the local population to surrender then he, in turn, left the town on 22nd July 1209. The town was captured and pillaged. The ransacking of Béziers is one of the major events in the crusade, even if the range of pillaging and the scope of the atrocities has been exaggerated.

above:

The Siege Stone.

Displayed in St. Nazaire's Cathedral in Carcassonne, it depicts the siege of the town by the crusaders.

gon, the Viscount of Carcassonne's sovereign, travelled to meet the princes and pleaded his vassal's cause. His attempt was unsuccessul and he soon left the country. In the end, Trencavel agreed to negotiate. He came to his enemies' camp with nine faithful followers and entered the Count of Nevers' tent where the crusade council was usually held. He was taken prisoner. This punishment is unusual under the laws of war. He may have sacrificed his own life in order to avoid his town suffering the same fate as Béziers. As soon as his surrender was announced, the people of Carcassonne left the walled town which was immediately occupied. This time, though, the Abbot of Cîteaux forbade any pillaging, threatening those who failed to obey him with excommunication.

Simon de Montfort

Young Trencavel's lands were confiscated. Again, this was a hard decision and it showed that the religious authorities had taken control, replacing any other power source and ignoring all feudal traditions. The problem then was to find a knight who would guard the lands. The greatest noblemen were embarrassed and refused the task, a thankless job for, as usual, any change of direction in military, political or diplomatic leadership could lead to the loss of the lands again. Finally, an Anglo-Norman nobleman, Simon de Montfort, accepted Arnaud Amaury's offer of Carcassonne, Béizers, Minerve and the Albi region. The character of de Montfort remains something of an enigma for there were those who hated him and others who admired him. He must have had a very steady faith, undoubted courage, undeniable tenacity and a very real talent for military matters. He was lord of Montfort (now Montfort-l'Amaury) near Paris but it is thought that he also owned the County of Leicester in England. From the outset, he asked the crusaders to be ready to come to his assistance if necessary. By this time, the crusade was running out of steam. The noblemen from the North had agreed to serve for forty days and they had no desire to remain in the South of France for a longer period. Only a small handful of noblemen remained with Simon de Montfort who gave Béziers to Guillaume de Contres and Limoux to Lambert de Crécy. Simon kept Carcassonne for himself; meanwhile, the Viscount died of dysentry in his prison cell on 10th November 1209. Montfort ordered a solemn funeral for him. Rumour had it that he had caused the death of the man whose lands he had seized but there is absolutely no proof of this.

As soon as the crusaders had moved on, Simon's companions found themselves in an untenable position and towns such as Montréal, Lombers or Castres regained their legitimate rulers. The people of Toulouse had refused to hand heretics over to the crusaders and the Count of Toulouse set off on a long journey to seek the political support of the King of France and the German Emperor, as well as the pardon of the Holy Father. He even agreed to entrust the citadel of Toulouse to the Abbot of Cîteaux who settled there. His preaching, though, had very little effect. "Oh, the old tom cat's purring," said the people of Toulouse, poking fun at the terrible prelate's soft voice.

Minerve and Termes

Simon de Montfort had succeeded in withstanding the winter months and, in June 1210, he set off to besiege and capture Minerve whose fortress was reputed to be impregnable. The siege lasted for seven weeks. The Abbot of Cîteaux laid down the conditions under which Guillaume de Minerve was to surrender. He was to leave the town with the Cathar believers and Perfects and all of them were to agree to be converted. The Abbot of Vaux-de-Cernay followed the crusaders when they entered the town and went to the Perfects' house. "We don't want your faith. We reject the Church of Rome". The women Perfects were equally firm. One hundred and forty Cathars who had refused to be converted were burnt at the stake. "Among these madmen are a few fine prostitutes," commented the author of the *Chanson*, cynically. Jean Duvernoy showed that Minerve was to be taken as a model for fifty years. "... The lords of Southern France were ready to defend the Perfects in their own castles. If forced to hand them over, they were also ready to abandon them to the victor. The Roman Catholic Church offered to spare the lives of those who agreed to be converted but the Perfects preferred the stake."

Minerve: the "candela". This slender tower is all that remains of Minerve Castle set on the highest part of the rock.

Termes: the crucial siege.
This 12th-century chapel serves as a reminder of the might of a family which gave enthusiastic support to the Cathar Perfects. The Siege of Termes was one of the most crucial events of the Albigensian Crusade.

Simon wanted to control the entire region and, in order to achieve his aim, besieged the castle in Termes. Guillaume de Contres brought in heavy weaponry, in particular the catapults that played such a vital part in weakening the walls of the citadels and the resistance of the defensive troops. The northern noblemen were harried by the barons of the South who had been dispossessed of their lands, the so-called *faidits*, who had found refuge in Cabaret. Termes resisted for four months because the castle stood in an outstanding location and had exceptional weaponry of its own. When the water tanks began to run dry, torrential rain fell and filled them up again. Unfortunately, an epidemic of dysentry broke out and the people besieged inside the citadel fled one night "by an underground passageway," according to the *Chanson*. The town fell on 23rd November 1210.

The offensive against the count of Toulouse

The Church strengthened its pressure on the Count of Toulouse, recalling the single authority of the King of France, meting out ever more punishments and constraints on the Count and his vassals and handing the lands over to the clergy or to Simon de Montfort. War between the crusaders and the Count was inevitable. The Count was assured of support from the Counts of Foix and Comminges. Bishop Foulque, who had tried to set up a brotherhood in Toulouse that would have been allied to the crusaders, was soon forced to join de Montfort. Any idea of a Count of Toulouse pardoned for his errors was disappearing fast.

Foulque again preached the crusade and the lords again answered his call and arrived in Southern France. They easily captured Cabaret then took Lavaur on 3rd May 1211. Again, 300 or 400 Perfects died at the stake, set up in a meadow. The leader of the town's defenders, Aimeri, Lord of Montréal, was hung with eighty knights and his sister, Dame Giraude was, "with her hands tied, thrown down a well. Her body was covered with a gravestone. This was a great sin for never, in all her life, had she let a pauper go without giving alms". During the Siege of Lavaur, Count Raimond Roger of Foix, a much-feared man of war, had succeeded in defeating 5,000 German crusaders. When Simon de Montfort laid siege to the castle in Les Cassès, he was on the Count of Toulouse' lands and Perfects who had refused to abjure were burnt at the stake. Count Baudoin, the Count of Toulouse' brother, handed Monferrand over to the crusaders. Simon de Montfort laid siege to Toulouse but soon gave up his attempt. After some of the crusaders had left, he was besieged in his turn by the Counts of Toulouse and Foix in Castelnaudary, a town with a reputation for being weak. However, the southern noblemen failed to take advantage of their superiority in numbers and a battle fought near the town remained indecisive. The *Chanson* recounts that the news of a victory by the Count of Toulouse spread like wild fire. In Lagrave, the population revolted and massacred the town's bailiff and the French garrison. It was Baudoin de Montferrand who, having rallied to the crusaders' cause, came to restore law and order. This revolt shows the extent of popular anger and the veritable loyalty to the Count of Toulouse when faced with threats from strangers, but the repression was instigated by the Count's own brother, himself a supporter of these "French-men". The Toulouse offensive had not succeeded in repulsing the barons of the North and ending a presence which, in the name of religion, was in fact an occupation, backed up by confiscations.

The defeat of Muret and the end of a dream

In April 1212, the crusaders returned and the chroniclers enjoyed emphasising the (no doubt exaggerated) diversity of their backgrounds. "... in huge companies came crusaders from Germany, Slavonia and Friesland, knights from Auvergne, and barons from Lombardy, all of them returned to do battle in a new crusade. Then the faction of Toulouse bowed low in fear, as if beneath a shower of rain..." On 1st December 1212, the statutes of Pamiers attempted to change the law in Occitania. Although Philip Augustus showed little interest in the Albigensian Crusade, it is probable that, in the minds of his counsellors, the idea of gradually bringing the South of France closer to the remainder of the kingdom was gaining ground.

The war took on a whole new dimension, through the intervention of the King of Aragon. He was basking in the splendour of his victory over the Moors of Spain in Andalusia, in Las Navas de Tolosa in July 1212. He had succeeded in reconquering his lands from the Moslems; now he wanted to make the best of the situation by regaining power to the north of the Pyrenees. He was further led to intervene by his family ties with the Count of Toulouse and his elder son, both of whom were his brothers-in-law. It goes without saying that there were close links between ordinary people and the princes, on both sides of the mountain range. Peter of Aragon was, though, equally worried about the political upheavals that were causing such changes in this border

Lastours. Views of Surdespine Castle, Tour Régine and, in the background, Cabaret Castle.

area between his kingdom and the kingdom of France. The alliance between Aragon and Toulouse was all the more dangerous because the crusaders' numbers were dwindling with every passing year. Peter of Aragon decided to besiege Muret, not far from Toulouse, which Simon de Montfort had just captured. The Count of Toulouse and his army joined him while Simon de Montfort arrived to set up camp within the town walls on 11th September 1213. Raimond VI wanted to put up palissades all round his camp; the Aragonese saw this as a mark of cowardice. The French barons therefore launched an attack against the Count of Toulouse' camp which was given support by the men of Aragon. However, two French soldiers succeeded in reaching the King of Aragon and killed him. Deprived of the backing of the knights of Aragon, the Count of Toulouse' army was disbanded. A good eye, a feeling for offensives, and organisational skills – these were the main advantages of Simon de Montfort who then appeared to be invincible. Raimond, meanwhile, sought refuge in Toulouse. The victory of Muret is an essential date in the history of Languedoc and Occitania, and in the history of France. According to Philippe Wolff, it sounded the death knell of any possible union between Aragon and Languedoc. The Pyrenees constituted a natural barrier, separating two different nations.

The defeat of the Count of Toulouse' army had major consequences. The papal legate, Pierre de Bénévent, obtained the submission of all the towns not previously held by de Montfort i.e. Narbonne, Toulouse, Foix, and the Comminges and Roussillon areas. Montfort then captured the Agen region, the southern borders of Périgord, and the Rouergue. In May 1215, the town of Toulouse submitted to the Church and to Simon. The King of France, Louis, who led a crusade from April to October 1215 was called upon for support. The Count of Toulouse and his son fled to England.

-----

opposite:

Fenouillet: a common destiny. One of the main preoccupations during the Early Middle Ages was the defence of the region against invasion by the Saracen. The areas around Peyrepertuse and Quéribus, like the Razès and Fenouillèdes regions, all suffered the same fate. The Carolingian monarchs transferred them to the Count of Barcelona, Wilfred the Hairy. One of his grandsons, Oliba Cabreta, was granted the Fenouillèdes and Peyrepertuse areas. Then it was the turn of his son, Bernard Taillefer, Count of Bésalù. Not until the Albigensian conflict in the 13th Century were the links with the princes on the other side of the Pyrenees finally severed.

The Tour Régine, one of the castles in Lastours.
This tower is roofed with a splendid dome and used to have a spiral staircase running up to the top.

Toulouse. The Dominicans' Cloisters (photo by Guy-Marie Renié).

Princes without lands

In November 1215, the Lateran Council met in Rome. The Church was going to re-organise Languedoc. Simon de Montfort was represented by his brother, Guy. The Count of Toulouse and his son were present, as was the Count of Foix. The latter was accused of being a bad Christian, of having a sister who was a Perfect, of having accepted her on his lands, and of permitting the fortification of Montségur, the "heretics' refuge". He replied that he had submitted to the Church on 18th April 1214, that he had handed over his awesome castle in Foix, and that he had "neither right nor power" over Montségur. He, in turn, attacked de Montfort, those who "dragged the Cross through the mud" and Bishop Foulque of Toulouse. The Pope promised him justice; he promised the same thing for Trencavel's son. The discussion turned to the question of Raimond. Should it be only lands belonging to heretics that were confiscated, when the dispossessed barons claimed that they were good Catholics? Was it possible to disinherit Raimond's son in recrimination for the errors of the father? The chronicler of the *Chanson*, who was a supporter of the Cathar cause, concluded, "The Princes of the Church forced the Holy Father to leave everything in de Montfort's greedy hands". In April 1216, the King of France confirmed the titles of Duke of Narbonne and Count of Toulouse on Simon de Montfort.

Simon's death

The Count of Toulouse and his son arrived in Provence, where they were given a warm welcome in Marseilles. Then Raimond received the submission of the town of Avignon. Philosopher Simone Weil admired the homage paid by a free town to a prince who had fallen from power and it is true that, in mediaeval society, the established order, hereditary rights and God-given traditions were all scrupulously respected. The Church and Simon de Montfort had upset society. The dispossessed lords, the *"faidits"*, were waiting for a signal before they came out of the shadows. Raimond VI travelled to Spain to raise an army while his son went to Beaucaire, which had been confiscated from the Count of Toulouse and given to de Montfort. A sworn enemy of de

THE CRUSADE OF SIMON DE MONTFORT

Simon de Montfort's death was totally unexpected. He had conquered Occitania in the name of the Church and seems always to have complied with the advice given to him by the prelates who accompanied him. He had given of his all in order to maintain control over towns and castles. The ecclesiastical authorities had not hesitated to dispossess barons who showed a degree of hesitation in their support or who were unruly. They acted in this way in order to satisfy the crusaders who had agreed to come south and in order to feed the troops. Simon's military talents had made this occupation possible, for a few years at least, but the solution was to prove fragile and temporary, always open to question, and it depended on one man. The idea began to be mooted of turning away from this heterogeneous collection of crusaders to a single, sovereign authority namely the King of France, who would send his son, Prince Louis, to lead the campaign. The crusade backed by the papacy and the prelates, the arrival of armies from throughout the Christian world and the range of religious motives involved gave way to a new logic – the strengthening of the position of the King of France.

After Simon de Montfort was killed at the Siege of Toulouse, his body was taken to Carcassonne for burial in St. Nazaire's Cathedral. His tombstone can still be seen there.

Montfort, troubadour Gui de Cavaillon accompanied the young Count. The town was taken, but not the castle that dominated it. Simon, who was trying to rekindle the spirit of the crusade in the North arrived with all due speed and set up camp near the town but he was unable to recapture it and he withdrew on 24th August 1216.

Simon returned to Toulouse where there was a groundswell of discontent. He quelled the disturbances by force. He had to carry out military campaigns, instigate sieges, and fight battles constantly in order to maintain the obedience of barons or towns whose only thought was to flee his authority. And, on 13th September 1217, he was unable to prevent Raimond VI from returning to Toulouse. The situation seemed particularly difficult and, once again, the prelates advised him to seek reinforcements from the North. De Montfort's wife, Alice de Montmorency, set off to ask for assistance from her brother, Mathieu de Montmorency, one of the heroes of the Battle of Bouvines. The reinforcements arrived in the spring of 1218. An attack was launched but Guy de Montfort was killed by an arrow and Simon was struck on the head by a stone. "It fell straight onto Simon de Montfort's steel helmet. His forehead was smashed, his jaw broken, and his brain and eyes sprung out of his head." Legend has it that the mangonel, the heavy weapon used to throw stones, was armed by a woman, or several women. The Siege of Toulouse was lifted and Simon's body was buried in the Cathedral Church of St. Nazaire in Carcassonne. According to the *Chanson*, the tombstone indicated clearly that Simon was "a saint and a martyr", a fact which greatly angered the poet.

The new logic: the king of France intervenes

Cardinal Bertrand, legate of Pope Honorius III, appointed Amaury de Montfort to succeed his father. Amaury benefitted from the assist-ance of Prince Louis who, having defeated the English and captured La Rochelle, arrived in Marmande. The besieged town was taken in 1219 and the population massacred. Amaury and Prince Louis headed for Toulouse but Louis of France abandoned the siege on 1st August 1219.

The Counts of Toulouse recaptured many strongholds such as Lavaur, Puylaurens, Montréal, and Mirepoix. Amaury de

-----

top to bottom:

Carcassonne. The stained-glass windows in the chevet of St. Nazaire's Cathedral.

Mirepoix. The interior of St. Maurice' Cathedral.

Montfort, who was indebted up to the hilt, transferred all his rights to the King of France and Prince Louis mounted the throne in 1223 under the title of King Louis VIII. Raimond VII became Count of Toulouse upon his father's death. And, in 1224, Amaury left Carcassonne to the young Raimond Trencavel. The Counts and barons of Southern France were confronted by a King of France who was fully acquainted with the Albigensian question. Furthermore, he was interested in it and determined to settle it once and for all. In December 1225, the Council of Bourges renewed the sentence passed on Raimond, enemy of Church and monarch alike.

Guilhabert de Castres

Despite the crusade, Catharism and the Cathar Church were still alive. From the first signs of impending trouble in the early 13th Century, the fortress of Montségur had been fortified. The Cathar Bishop, Gaucelm, and his "major son" Guilhabert de Castres sought refuge there during the crusade. The fortress appeared to be the centre of Catharism and a means of guaranteeing its survival.

The barons from the North had failed to achieve a final victory over the heresy, despite burning followers at the stake and confiscating property. The barons of Southern France returned to their lands with the agreement of the King of France and hastened to provide the Perfects with protection again. Guilhabert de Castres built a house for himself in Fanjeaux. Women Perfects who had sought refuge in convents or priories then turned them into Cathar convents. A new era of tolerance seemed to be arriving. The Count of Toulouse gave his protection to the nuns of Prouille. Meetings brought Cathars and Roman Catholics face to face. Great efforts were made by the "Good Christians" who had survived the crusade to reorganise their Church. Bernard de Lamothe, for example, travelled extensively through the region before being ordained as a Cathar Bishop. He attended a veritable council in Pieusse in 1226 at which almost one hundred Perfects were present and at which it was decided to designate a bishop for the Razès area around Limoux.

The driving force behind this reconstruction was Guilhabert de Castres. He was the man who had welcomed Esclarmonde of Foix into the Cathar Church and it was he who had attended the debate at Montréal. He sought refuge in Montségur and turned to the nobility of Catalonia for assistance. In 1221, he met two of the great feudal lords of the Pyrenees in Mirepoix for this very purpose. Taking advantage of the lull in hostilities he began to preach openly in the lowlands, but the renewed offensive by the royal army forced him to flee. The King of France launched a major campaign in 1226. Avignon was captured, contrary to all expectations. The king, in fact, met with very little resistance. People flocked to join his army, especially as the Cathars were subject to fierce repressionary measures. The Cathar bishop of the Carcassonne area, Pierre Isarn, was burnt at the stake in front of Louis VIII's own eyes. When the king left the area, Imbert de Beaujeu was commissioned to take over as commander-in-chief of his army, a royal fighting force that had acquired a sense of coherence and that rampaged through the entire region meting out punishment to heretics. The Perfects of Labécède were burnt at the stake in July 1227. Although Louis VIII died shortly afterwards, his widow, Blanche of Castile, continued the struggle in Southern France, on behalf of the young Louis IX. Her family background caused her quite naturally to turn her attention to the South and to attempt to force it to its knees.

Raimond VII had been in danger as the king's army advanced for the Count of Foix had abandoned him to his fate and

-----

Puilaurens: stone lookouts.

In the fortress in Puilaurens, only the square tower, or keep, was built before the start of the crusade, probably in the 12th Century.

Limoux.

The Chapel of Our Lady of Marceille.

many of the barons rallied to the royal cause. Yet the Count succeeded in slackening the grip of the monarchy over the next few years. Jean Duvernoy underlined the paradoxical nature of the situation. Noblemen whose entire families had been won over to Catharism and who had themselves given the religion their support submitted to the King of France. Among them was Bernard-Oth de Niort whose grandmother, mother and aunts had all been Perfects yet who declared himself loyal to the sovereign. Olivier and Bernard de Termes, whose father had courageously defended the family citadel and who had, for many years, fought on behalf of the Count of Toulouse, handed their castle over to the King of France, but retained their other lands by paying homage to the monarch (November 1228). Behind all these oaths of loyalty, there was the shadow of fear, and the fatigue that follows years of warfare; there was also recognition of the authority of the King of France, an authority that was no longer open to doubt and which guaranteed order and peace. In the eyes of the monarchy, it was vital to save the social order, the nobility of Southern France and local freedoms – to do so, the Albigensian sect would be sacrificed.

The count of Toulouse submits to the king

It was doubtless in this frame of mind that Raimond agreed to negotiate with Blanche of Castile who was assisted by Cardinal Romain de Saint-Ange. Raimond travelled to Meaux and signed the Treaty of Meaux and Paris on 12th April 1229. The conditions imposed upon him were draconian indeed. He was to remain loyal to king and Church and clear his lands of heresy. He was to pay anybody who was prepared to help him uncover a heretic. He was forbidden to give official posts to anybody suspected of having connections with the Cathars. He was to give back to the Church the property that it owned prior to the crusade and pay a very heavy indemnity. Normally, he was to go on a Crusade to the Holy Land, but this he dispensed with. He treated as friends all those who had declared themselves in favour of the crusaders. He dismantled his fortresses and handed over to the king any that were not dismantled. The treaty laid down the new borders of the county. Raimond was to retain the Toulouse area for the rest of his life, except for

Toulouse.

The chevet of the Basilica Church of Saint-Sernin (photo by Guy-Marie Renié).

Mirepoix which was given to Guy de Lévis, Marshal of the "Army of Faith". The Count, on the other hand, acquired the much-coveted Lauragais area, kept the Agen area and Rouergue, and still owned part of the dioceses of Cahors and Albi. He consented to the marriage of his daughter and heiress, Jeanne, with the king's brother, Alphonse of Poitiers, and she brought her husband vast territories as part of her dowry. If Jeanne and Alphonse had no children, the king of France would be their heir. The Count transferred to the Pope all his lands to the East of the Rhône, i.e. Avignon and the Comtat Venaissin. To the West of the Rhône, the territories occupied by the royal troops formed the senechalsies of Beaucaire, Carcassonne, Béziers and Nîmes. Amaury de Montfort abandoned all his rights in the South of France but was promised the title of Constable of the Realm.

Raimond's absolution by the Church was marked by a ceremony on the steps of Notre-Dame in Paris. Dressed in his shirt, the Count knelt before the papal legate. He returned to Toulouse in November 1229. The Count of Foix also submitted. This submission roused the indignation of historians in the South. "He had really defeated Simon de Montfort and had not abdicated before Louis VIII. What circumstances led to the sad sight that was then to be offered to us? Why, when he left Languedoc unvanquished if not an outright victor, was he to return after having handed over his lands, bound and gagged, to the king and the Church" (Fernand Niel). This indignation hides a form of patriotism, one might almost say nationalism, linked to the love of a country – Languedoc or Occitania. This, though, is perhaps an anachronism. Men were not connected to a region or a locality so much as to a person, a lineage, and a family whose history was entwined with the history of the region or locality. The Count of Toulouse sacrificed himself in order to resume a history that had been interrupted by the Albigensian crusade. The hierarchies of the mediaeval world were an important factor and they were seen by their contemporaries as immovable, as a reflection of the celestial world. In order to regain his normal, ancient place in society, the Count had to recognise the supremacy of the Church and, thereafter, of the king. Henry II Plantagenet was equally humiliated by the murder of Thomas Becket. Georges Duby prudently resituated the Treaty of Meaux in its historical context when discussing the *Chanson*, "The force of his outburst should not mask the fact that it was to Raymond VII, after he had reconciled himself with the Church and promised to fight Catharism with his every last breath, that the young King Louis IX returned the county, in 1229. None of his advisers would have felt it right to annex the lands to the royal estates; indeed none of them would have deemed it profitable to do so. It is true that the sovereign retained Carcassonne, Beaucaire and the surrounding areas, but he did so in order to ensure against a possible U-turn on the part of the Count of Toulouse, to build an advanced post in the fight against Catharism and, more especially, to guarantee himself an opening to the sea and, consequently, to the real Crusades, the ones that took place in the Holy Land." Gérard Sivéry, biographer of Blanche of Castile, wrote, "The king, then, was the winner. The Count of Toulouse accepted defeat but retained a large part of his possessions, a source of regret among his fiercest enemies. They then launched a new campaign of denigration against Blanche of Castile, constantly accusing her of protecting her cousin, Raimond VII, to the detriment of the interests of Louis IX's loyal vassals in the South of France".

The founding of the Inquisition

The Treaty of Meaux was soon followed by a council in Toulouse at which the destiny of the heretics was to be decided once the political questions had been solved. It was there-fore decided, in November 1229, that each parish would have a committee consisting of a priest and two or three lay people who would be responsible for seeking out and denouncing heretics. The noblemen were to join in this search and would be punished if they failed to do so. However, the council ordered that nobody could be condemned as a heretic without having been judged as such by a bishop or other ecclesiastical authority. In 1231, the Pope reconfirmed that only the Church was entitled to condemn somebody on grounds of heresy. And the word "inquisitor", with its new meaning, appeared in the statutes drawn up by a senator in Rome. This marked the birth of the Inquisition, a task entrusted to followers of St. Dominic, the Dominicans, under the terms of the papal bull *Ille humani generis* of 8th February 1232. From then on, the Count of Toulouse legally enforced the decisions taken by Gregory IX. Heretics were sought out by men of the word, preachers whose strong intellectual training enabled them to debate theological subtleties and whose exemplary lifestyle did not leave scope for anticlerical criticisms. Gradually, they replaced the bishops and secular clergy in this pursuit of bad Christians,

since the original committees had been suspected of complaisance and weakness. In April 1233, the Pope asked the Provincial of the Dominicans to appoint two brothers who would pass judgement with full powers and without any right to appeal. The Dominicans depended only on Rome, which reinforced their power still further, and this enabled them to attack high-ranking people, including a number of great noblemen. They sought out heretics in the very heart of abbeys. They had no hesitation in demanding the exhumation of heretics so that their bodies could be burned. The Inquisition developed a fearsome method of enquiry that was meticulous, rigourous and pitiless. This model became a symbol of repression but people were not sentenced on grounds of heresy until there had been a scrupulous investigation and the discovery of absolute proof. In Northern France, the Pope appointed a former Perfect, Robert the Bogomil, as Inquisitor General; he proved to be totally ruthless and was eventually disavowed. In the South, it was one of Dominic's companions, Pierre Sellan, who was appointed with Brother Guillaume Arnaud and, later, Arnaud Catala.

The eagles' nests

The Perfects had left the villages in 1229. Thereafter, they could only count on noblemen, who had castles built at the very summits of mountains, for support and shelter. A large group headed by Guilhabert de Castres begged Raimond de Péreille to given them shelter in his citadel at Montségur where the heretic Church would have its "seat and its head". There, Guilhabert proceeded with ordinations. From there he sent out his deacons and Perfects and it was there, too, that he defended them.

Knights settled in Montségur with their equerries, living off the treasure trove belonging to the Cathar Church. The treasure was amassed thanks to believers who made bequests when they were on their death beds or who asked their heirs to do so on their behalf. The money was also used to pay barons who agreed to protect the Perfects in return for payment.

Soon, the Cathars became used to a nomadic lifestyle for they had to flee the ever-present threats facing them. When

-----

The cloisters in Fontfroide Abbey: the Cistercians combat the heresy. The monks lived in isolated spots and this abbey is well off the beaten track. The Order of Cîteaux breathed new life into the old Benedictine Order and it was the Cistercians who began fighting the heresy that their spiritual leader, St. Bernard, had discovered in the South of France.

the Perfects described their lives to the Inquisitors, they told of constant travelling from shelter to shelter, from house to castle, and from caves to forests. The Inquisitors even appointed specialists to seek out these shelters, leaders, guides and messengers *(ductores, receptatores, nuncii)*. A whole mysterious world was opened up before them, a world of despair. Raimond VII and the Bishop of Toulouse, a Dominican, took part in the search for Cathars and arrested a number of Perfects. The Inquisitors sought out Cathars in Toulouse itself, with the assistance of an Italian brother, Roland of Cremona. On 4th August 1234, the day on which St. Dominic was canonised, Bishop Raimond of Toulouse heard that a Cathar woman nearing death was about to receive the *consolamentum*. After Mass, the prelate went to her house, omitted to tell her he was a bishop, and waited until the dying woman, mistaking his identity, confessed to her secret faith. The old woman was taken, on her death bed, to the stake. Then the entire Dominican convent went for a meal in the refectory. Such acts, especially exhumations, caused anger among the townspeople who criticised the Inquisitors and the Dominicans in general. At the end of 1235, the people of Toulouse chased the Inquisitors, the Dominicans and the Bishop out of their town. A new form of solidarity began to grow up between the noblemen who had been dispossessed on grounds of heresy and the Perfects who were being pursued. This solidarity slowly became anchored deep in society, as if the number of believers increased in proportion to the level of persecutions. As to the Count of Toulouse, he swithered. He supported the Inquisition and his men even managed to capture a leading Cathar in Montségur. In 1233, the Count showed himself to be a zealous Catholic, taking measures against those who murdered informers. He ordered the sealing up of isolated huts, subterranean passages, and caves, all of them places of refuge for Cathars on the run. Yet, at the same time, the Count sought ways of lightening the burden on the heretics among his people.

The attack in Avignonet

Tension was running so high that, in 1240, the Trencavels' heir crossed the Pyrenees with the agreement of the Count of Foix. Troops came down the Upper Aude Valley, were assisted by the dispossessed nobility (the *"faidits"*) and the Perfects were again able to preach in Fanjeaux. The Count of Toulouse, though, remained prudent and he gave no open support to the Viscount. The town of Carcassonne did

not surrender. It was well defended by the King of France's Seneschal, Guillaume des Ormes. In the end, Trencavel was besieged in Montréal and it took the intervention of the Counts of Toulouse and Foix to get him out. A royal army pursued the rebels and, on 16th November 1240, the Lord of Peyrepertuse, having completed negotiations which eradicated the past, surrendered his impregnable citadel to King Louis IX's troops.

The Count of Toulouse' offensive was much more worrying for the King of France and the Church. Raimond VII had renewed his submission to Louis IX on 14th March 1241 in Montargis and had promised to be-siege Montségur. In fact, he limited his action to a display of military might at the foot of the citadel. On the other hand, he set up a military coalition with the kings of Castile, Navarre, Aragon and England, and even included Trencavel. He told his subjects

opposite:

Bouan: refuge in the caves.

Some of the caves were given fortifications; like the "spoulga" in Bouan which still has its crenelations. Many of these shelters have given rise to legends such as the initiation ceremonies said to have been performed in Bethléem or the tales referring to the cave at Lombrives where Cathars are said to have been walled up alive.

-----

above:

Avignonet-Lauragais: defying the Inquisition.

The Lauragais area was profoundly affected by the heresy and a Cathar council is said to have met at Saint-Félix. The murder carried out in Avignonet shows the extent to which an entire population could become involved, in the face of the terrifyingly powerful Inquisition. A painting in the church shows the Inquisitors and martyrs arriving in Heaven.

that he wanted to shake off the obligations incumbent upon him under the terms of the Treaty of Meaux.

In order to mobilise the Cathar knights, he allowed "deeds most foul" to be perpetrated in Avignonet. *Faidits* travelled down from Montségur, headed by Pierre-Roger of Mirepoix, and were soon joined by other soldiers. In all, the group consisted of eighty people. With the complicity of one of the Count's illegitimate nephews, they entered Avignonet after pretending to beat down the gates. Once inside, they murdered the Inquistors (a Dominican and a Franciscan), an archdeacon and their entourage, a total of ten people. This was a premeditated act and other knights awaited the Inquisitors elsewhere in case they succeeded in escaping.

The threat was fully understood by Blanche of Castile and by the Church. Henry of England landed in Royan and the Count of la Marche attacked. Louis IX fought back, vigourously. The

Montségur, the Sacred Refuge.

Battles of Taillebourg and Saintes in July 1242 forced the English to retreat to Bordeaux. Raimond VII, who had been excommunicated for his complicity in the Avignonet massacre, had acquired the support of Nîmes, Albi, the Razès area and the Termes region but the royal troops still held Carcassonne and Béziers. The Count's position soon became untenable and he sought pardon from the future St. Louis, who was more concerned with leaving a kingdom at peace with itself before setting off on a Crusade. Raimond of Toulouse was allowed to travel to Rome to ask the Pope to lift his excommunication.

The fall of Montségur

The royal army was free to seek revenge for the attack on the Inquisition. Montségur was the key to the resistance to the king and the Church and, as such, had to be captured. The garrison consisted of some three hundred and forty people, led by Pierre-Roger de Mirepoix and Raimond de Péreille, his first cousin and father-in-law. There were 160 lay people including 27 women and 20 sergeants, and 180 Perfects. Guilhabert de Castres was dead; he had been succeeded by Bertrand Marty. It is difficult to imagine what the castle looked like at that time, for it has doubtless been altered since then. However, Montségur was a difficult place to supply with food and water.

The siege began in the spring of 1243. It was led by Seneschal Hugues des Arcis of Carcassonne, accompanied by Pierre Amiel, the Archbishop of Narbonne, and the Bishop of Albi. Because of the lie of the land, it was impossible to cut the fortress off – a number of audacious men managed to slip into the castle regularly to take in news from outside. Eventually, it was Gascons who climbed the mountain at night and succeeded in capturing a look-out post. The Bishop of Albi, a skilful engineer of heavy weaponry, set up a catapult which sent stones raining down on the people inside the castle. Another engineer, Bertrand de Capdenac, succeeded in entering Montségur. However, on 1st March 1244, Pierre-Roger de Mirepoix surrendered. He had negotiated the surrender and requested that the lay people be allowed to go free, but he handed over the Perfects who had to choose between abjuring their faith and being burnt at the stake. Almost two hundred of them died in the flames. "The fall of Montségur was a symbol. Yet even though it marked the disappearance of the most consummate "monastery" complete with hierarchy, a "Mother Superior" of women Perfects, houses and monthly "services", it did little to change the preaching habits of the many "clergy" still operating underground" (Jean Duvernoy).

The Fenouillet area was still putting up resistance, thanks to its admirable citadels in Quéribus, Puylaurens, and Fenouillet. This was of political importance because the Cathars sought refuge there. It was also of strategic importance in a border area such as this, for these eagles' nests controlled Carcassonne, which the king was then required to defend. Olivier de Termes had surrendered Aguilar before setting off for the Holy Land; he was to become one of St. Louis' closest advisers. Trencavel, who had also been pardoned after waiving all his rights, followed the king on the Crusades and was granted land in the Corbières area. The dynasty then died out.

When Olivier de Termes returned from the Crusades, he succeeded in capturing Chabert de Barbeira who was holding Quéribus and in obtaining the surrender of the stronghold. And in 1258, the Treaty of Corbeil was signed by France and James I of Aragon who obtained official recognition of his authority over Roussillon, Cerdagne and Catalonia and who, in return, abandoned his claims to Béziers, Albi, Carcassonne, Nîmes, the Lauragais area and the Gévaudan. He did, however, retain Montpellier. As to Alphonse of Poitiers, he had taken possession of Toulouse with his wife, in 1249 on the death of Raimond VII and, as he had no children, he prepared to hand the county over to direct rule by the King of France. The European prestige of the monarch, the future St. Louis, and the prosperity enjoyed in the 13th Century were no doubt instrumental in enabling the people of Occitania to accept these changes. Historical evolution did the rest and Occitania turned its attention to France. Georges Duby emphasised this fact, "It was even more difficult to believe that, in Languedoc which was then annexed to the crown by pure chance, the influence of Paris, the desire for a career, and a will to live the same life as people at Court and speak the monarch's language would quickly lead the Occitanian culture to die out".

Resistance to the Inquisition

It was the Inquisition who destroyed the last clandestine Cathars. At the same time it drew up its own rules and regulations, turning them into veritable manuals. One of the oldest of these books was written between 1244 and 1254 by four Dominicans who had operated in Languedoc. And it was an Inquisitor from the Toulouse region, Bernard

Gui, who wrote the most famous of all these works, *Practica inquisitionis* in 1320. The procedure was always the same. Suspects were asked to acknowledge their heresy; this was a time of grace. Penitence would then be mild and secret. After a month, any heretics who had not admitted to their faults could no longer hope for clemency. They were served with a writ to appear before the Inquisition. If they refused, they were to be arrested by civilian authorities. The suspect's interrogation was carried out in the presence of two members of the Church, with the assistance of a notary and a clerk who took down the statements made. The Inquisitor could use guile to try and obtain a confession. All these practices were early forms of methods now used by the police today. Two witnesses were all that was required to prove that a suspect was indeed a heretic and the Inquisition encouraged informers. In order to obtain a confession, it was often deemed useful to leave the suspect in prison for some considerable time. The Pope, in a bull entitled *Ad extirpanda* issued in 1252, authorised torture i.e. whipping, the rack, strappado, and the use of hot coals but stressed that torture should not result in mutilation and, more particularly, should not cause death. By showing the instruments of torture to a suspect, the Inquisitors sought to strike fear into him or her and thereby obtain a confession. Sentences handed down included a term of imprisonment, the confiscation of property, and, for impenitent or relapsed heretics, the death penalty. The Church was not entitled to take life; it "abandoned" heretics to the secular arm of the law and they were burnt at the stake. Sometimes they were strangled before being thrown into the fire. As regards imprisonment or *murus*, a distinction was made between imprisonment in a dark dungeon and a more liberal regime. Those found guilty of heresy were also submitted to humiliation as a form of punishment, such as the wearing of yellow Crosses on their clothes.

These procedures caused anger among ordinary people and, because of the secrecy in which they were cloaked, struck terror into the hearts of all. The methods used by the Inquisition did not really seem to guard against sentencing innocents, but they did seem to be arbitrary. In deciding to confiscate the property of condemned people, the Inquisitors could have motives that were far from spiritual. In 1283, a conspiracy occurred in Carcassonne. Attempts were made to obtain the list of suspects held by the Inquisition's Court. In 1296, the Inquisitors even turned their attention to the mendicant friars, the Franciscans (or Grey Friars).

Inquisitor Nicolas d'Abbeville and the Bishop of Albi continued as they had begun. In the early 1300's, a major Court case took place in Albi at which 35 leading personalities were questioned and 25 of them sentenced to imprisonment. The population revolted, booed the bishop and circulated bogus lists of suspects in order to make the Inquisitors'

Montségur.

– This stone serves as a reminder of the last Cathars burnt at the stake when Montségur Castle fell.

– The spur of limestone rock in the part of the Pyrenees lying within Ariège, which rises to a height of 3,923 ft. and is topped by Montségur Castle, is commonly known as a "pog".

task more difficult. The revolt found itself a leader in one Bernard Délicieux, a reader in theology at the Franciscan Friary in Carcassonne. He embodied the protests raised against the arbitrary behaviour of the Inquisition. King Philip the Fair was shaken by the accusations made against the Inquisitors, especially as he was himself engaged in conflict with the papacy in Rome. He had the Inquisition's procedures suspended but, in 1303, a Dominican became Pope under the name of Benedict XI and he had every confidence in the members of his Order. The matter took on political overtones. The Southern French turned to the son of the King of Aragon for assistance and Bernard Délicieux was involved in the negotiations. This was more than the King of France could bear. He ordered the hanging of all the burghers who were involved in the plot. Forty of them died in Limoux, fifteen in Carcassonne. The Inquisition regained its rights and Bernard Délicieux was imprisoned and tortured. In 1307, Bernard Gui was appointed to Toulouse as the town's Inquisitor and he observed that the Cathars had returned. "During this persecution of the Inquisitors and the disturbances to the work of the Holy Office, many Perfects attended meetings and they began to gather strength (heresies were rife)." From 1299 onwards, Catharism enjoyed renewed popularity thanks to the action of the Authié brothers (Pierre was a lawyer in Ax-les-Thermes). Repression, however, was systematic and brutal. The Inquisition, freed of the attacks that had been made against it and the lack of confidence expressed by both Paris and Rome, was able to take action and it eradicated this renewal of faith in just a few years.

Montaillou, an occitanian village

The village of Montaillou was being watched by the Inquisition. It was also subject to the vigilance of the Bishop of Pamiers. In 1317, Jacques Fournier was appointed Bishop and he made use of a decision taken by the Council of Vienne in 1312 by which episcopal authority could be associated with the Inquisition and its Courts. Before then, the Inquisition had always operated alone. Jacques Fournier worked with a Dominican named Gaillard de Pomiès, himself appointed by the head of the Inquisition in Carcassonne. Until 1326, when he became Bishop of Mirepoix, Jacques Fournier headed the investigations aimed at stamping out the Cathar heresy. From 1318 to 1325, the Court sat for 370 days and carried out 578 interrogations. This work led to the *Register of Pamiers* which was studied by a number of scholars. It was edited, in its entirety, by Jean Duvernoy in 1965 and formed the basis of the magnificent work by Emmanuel Le Roy Ladurie published in France in 1975, *Montaillou, an Occitan Village*. Those suspected of heresy lived in the highlands around Foix, the Sabarthès area and, in Montaillou itself, 25 people were accused.
Here, as elsewhere at the beginning of the 14th Century, the Inquisition's procedures were well-regulated. They began with statements from informants. The suspect was served with a writ to appear before the Court, sometimes by the parish priest during his homily. If the suspect refused to attend the hearing, the local Bailiff arrested him or her. Brought before the judges, the suspect then had to take an oath on the Gospels and answer the detailed questions put by the Inquisitors. Sometimes suspects were imprisoned, sometimes they were placed under house-arrest, and sometimes

THE « FOUR GREAT DEVILS »

Le Roy Ladurie described four powers that were influential in Montaillou. The local lord was none other than the Count of Foix, represented in Montaillou by a castellan who had a military function and by a bailiff who had legal authority. The second power was the Inquisition from Carcassonne which had "servants" to carry out its orders although it was also backed up by its own lawyers, jailers, and agents scattered throughout the population, in particular among the clergy. The third power was the Bishop of Pamiers who controlled the hierarchy of the priest-hood and monitored the always difficult task of obtaining the payment of tithes. Finally, the fourth power was the distant kingdom of France, which was feared and hated. The Count of Foix was a vassal of the sovereign. A royal army could come at any time and defend the Established Church. This confirmed the changes instigated by the Treaty of Meaux, "As a final resort, French forces are far away but they are efficient and the threat posed by them hangs like the sword of Damocles over the hotheads of the Sabarthès area." Bélibaste, a Cathar, summarised the hatred of the Cathars in the following terms, "There are four great devils controlling the world – the main devil is the Pope whom I call Satan, the second is the King of France, the third is the Bishop of Pamiers, and the fourth is the Inquisitor of Carcassonne."

they were excommunicated. In some cases, to force them to confess, the Inquisition had them thrown into a dark, narrow dungeon, clapped in irons and fed on black bread and water. Torture was not used by Jacques Fournier; he was content to use police methods to seek out religious deviants through evidence from their everyday lives. This document is of inestimable value, for Jacques Fournier was to become Pope in Avignon in 1334 under the name of Benedict XII.

Le Roy Ladurie's study gives an insight into Catharism, or to be more precise the temptation to embrace Catharism, as a part of everyday life. In the 1290's, the castellan was Bérenger de Roquefort whose wife was Béatrice de Planissoles. Her father had been obliged to wear the yellow Cross and, as a young girl, Béatrice had been attracted by the arguments of the Cathars. At one time, she wanted to travel to Lombardy, where the heretics sought refuge, with her Intendant who was in love with her. She was raped then had an affair with Pierre Clergue, the parish priest in Montaillou who was a Cathar and who tried to convince her to join the movement; he was also a double agent, working for the Inquisition. She was remarried, widowed, then lived with an unimportant vicar of the parish to whom she was even married without receiving the nuptial benediction. She was arrested by the Inquisition, freed but sentenced to wear the yellow Cross.

Her former lover, Pierre Clergue, was the bailiff's brother and a very colourful character. His charm worked wonders on women, who were unable to resist him, often with the consent of their husbands or mothers. The priest supported Cathar ideas and, for a long time, was able to use his connections with the Court in Foix or within the Church to ward off the dangers threatening his neighbours or friends. "Ah, if only all the parish priests in the world were like the one in

Montaillou!" sighed a Cathar missionary in 1301. He even set aside part of the tithes to help the Good Men. At the same time, however, he was one of the Inquisition's informants and this forced him to become the local instrument of the Inquisitors. He had no hesitation in taking revenge on enemy families. The mass arrests of August 1308 were dramatic. The entire population of Montaillou was arrested except for the children, during the Feast of the Blessed Virgin Mary. A few of the inhabitants went to the stake; others spent many long years in prison. The remaining population returned to the village which was under the control of the Clergue faction; everybody was obliged to wear a yellow Cross. However, Pierre Clergue was confronted in his turn with a redoubtable adversary in the person of Jacques Fournier who had him imprisoned in 1320. Like his brother, he died there. Through in-depth knowledge of the families, the Inquisitor and, later, the historian were able to describe the faith of these people. First and foremost, Le Roy Ladurie showed that magic and superstition were less important than were once thought. On the other hand, the main question was salvation and this was where the Good Men brought their own answer, a different response to the one provided by the Roman Catholic Church. There were many who hesitated between orthodoxy and heterodoxy and who attempted to reconcile Catholic tradition and respect for the Cathars. There were many who wanted to "get the best of both worlds". According to Roman Catholic law, the confession made to a priest was the only way of removing sins. On the other hand, the Cathars despised the clergy and, at the time of death, offered people the *consolamentum* which eradicated all faults and sins in one fell swoop while, at the same time, ensuring salvation. At the beginning of the 14th Century, the *endura* completed this ritual preparation for the other world. People at death's door wanted to be sure of their salvation and avoid committing any more sins. They therefore sought death by refusing to eat. They also chased away the parish priest and insulted him if he wanted to approach the deathbed.

The people of the Sabarthès area were best acquainted with the *Pater noster*, even though, normally, it was the Perfects who said this prayer for they alone were on the path to Truth. The villagers were accustomed to making the sign of the Cross over food or over the bed, even though the Cathars did not like the Cross, which they saw as a shameful symbol of Christ's humanity. They referred to the Saviour, often confusing Him with God. And it is more than likely that this Christ was no longer the Christ of the Romanesque era, triumphant on the day of the Last Judgement. Instead, He was a man who went through suffering, as He did throughout the Christian world. This image tended to contradict the Cathar's refusal to consider Christ as a man, i.e. a creature of Evil. The villagers in the Sabarthès took Holy Communion, although some of them made fun of the piece of "biscuit" or "cake". They loved the Virgin Mary and repeated the *Ave Maria* even though the Good Men told them that it was worthless, a prayer invented by the clergy. And so, despite the respect that most people had for the Cathars, those suspected of heresy retained the appearance of Catholicism – even if they then removed the veil of untruth when they were approaching death. During confession, they were careful not to acknowledge their confidence in the Cathar faith.

Their support, however, had an effect on their everyday lives. "The shepherds of Montaillou are happy to discuss theology". And Dualism is then apparent. Spirits, seduced by the Devil, have fallen to Earth. They await final redemption by passing from one body to another, occasionally taking the form of animals. This concept of metempsychosis strengthened the power of the Perfects who granted final salvation to the soul via the *consolamentum*. In everyday life, there was also the *melioramentum*, a blessing given by the Good Men to those who "adored" them. Le Roy Ladurie concluded, "In my view, there is no doubt that, in Montaillou, Catharism was seen, by those who had embraced this faith, as an extreme and heroic variation of Christianity and not as a non-Christian religion." A Perfect saves those who venerate him and his personal virtues are sufficient to ensure this salvation. A Perfect does not lie, does not eat meat or cheese, does not sleep with women, and does not take gold or silver from others. A Perfect is a holy man who acts as an intercessor, "the leader of a small secret society within the village".

------

left:

Albi. The Berbie Palace,

now the Toulouse-Lautrec Museum, used to the residence of the Bishops of Albi (photo by Jeanne Duprat).

right:

Pamiers. Entrance to St. Antonin's Cathedral.

Liberty and fear

This had an effect on ordinary morality. Since the ultimate pardon was granted by the Good Men, sins were less important and sexual morality was, if not depraved, at least much less constrained. Father Pierre Clergue set an example. Since the sexual act, even in marriage, was a sin in the eyes of the Cathars, all rules are of equal value and it is acceptable not to comply with any of them. For a small number of women who found pleasure in the sexual act, this was no longer a sin. And since confession was meaningless for the Cathars, it was useless to go and recount such pranks to the parish priest!

This apparent liberty, though, cost them dear for the Inquisition was watching. Everyday life was made up of dissimulation, concealment, discreet messengers, and rapid escapes into the mountains. People also had to be careful not to speak too much for words, even if spoken several years before, could be used as proof of heresy. Complaisance with regard to the Cathar faith, loyalty to the Perfects whose words reassured and consoled, and confidence in the salvation that they promised meant looking over one's shoulder every minute of the day.

The last known Perfect, Guillaume Bélibaste, was the son of a wealthy farmer and he had killed a shepherd. He served his noviciate in Rabastens and received the *consolamentum*. When his life was threatened, he took refuge in Catalonia but he returned to France and was arrested in 1321. He was burnt at the stake in Villerouge-Termenès.

And the Inquisition, through its meticulous investigations and cruelty, finally succeeded in wiping out the heresy, which disappeared in the 14th Century.

The metamorphoses of the Cathar idea

The heresy intrigued people over the centuries that followed its extinction. For many years, it was associated with, if not assimilated to, the Waldensian movement whose last few followers survived in the alpine valleys of the Piedmont. In the 17th Century, Bossuet became interested in the Cathars and the Waldenses, seeing them as the ancestors of the Protestants. It was, indeed, a Protestant theologian from Strasbourg, Charles Schmidt, who began the first real scholarly research into the Cathar religion. One of his main sources was the Doat Collection of handwritten registers kept in the national library in Paris. It was under the direction of Councillor Doat that Colbert had had copies made of the Languedoc archives. This scholarly tradition has developped and grown in proportion until the present day, as can be seen in the admirable *Cahiers de Fanjeaux*.

From the 19th Century onwards, the persecution of the Cathars nourished differing streams of thought. On one hand, there was the anticlericalism which was seeking examples of the cruelty of the Established Church and which found in the Inquisition a model of intolerance. In some cases, anticlericalism was linked to the rediscovery of the literature of the troubadours and, through them, the celebration of the Occitan civilisation, its language (a direct descendent of Latin) and its poetry. Yet the Cathars had already become a choice literary theme for the Romantics. A Hungarian writer, Niklaus Lenau, published a long poem called "The Albigensians" in 1838. But it was Napoléon Peyrat, a minister in the Reformed Church, who created the

------

opposite:

Cabaret Castle in Lastours: memories of Pierre-Roger.

Pierre-Roger de Cabaret was one of the Trencavels' companions-in-arms, as well as their vassal. His whole life was affected by the Cathar faith, which he protected without ever joining it. Here in the keep there is ribbed vaulting but it is difficult to put a date on the various buildings.

Villerouge-Termenès and memories of Bélibaste.

Guillaume de Bélibaste's family were all Cathars. Guillaume, who was born in 1280, killed a shepherd who wanted to denounce him and his parents to the authorities. He is considered as the last Perfect. When he was discovered, he was imprisoned in Carcassonne before being burnt at the stake in Villerouge in 1321.

golden legend surrounding the Cathars, "The barons lived in keeps on bare hilltops. Their mothers and sisters lived the life of recluses in caves above jagged slopes on the shores of mountain streams…. The castle afforded protection for the caves; the caves prayed for the keeps…" This was how the minister described his arrival at Montségur, "I salute you, I cried, weeping, Sacred gate, house of the Pure, residence of the Perfects, sanctuary of the Gospels and Romanic country!" Napoléon Peyrat saw the Cathars as Johannines, i.e. faithful followers of St. John, and it was he who placed Montségur at the forefront of Catharism in Occitania. "… An Essenean Sion, a platonic Delphi set in the Pyrenees, a Johannine Rome, banished and wild, set down in Aquitaine. Montségur, from its deserted rock, looked firmly but sadly across to the Louvre and the Vatican, the King of France and the Pope of Rome… In its cave, it concealed three irreconcilable enemies of theocracy – Speech, Homeland and Freedom, all of them forces for the future."

Anticlericalism gained strength during the Third Republic and politicians who were hostile to the Church had no hesitation in quoting the terrible phrase, "Kill them all; God will recognise His own!" Historians and writers also tried to bring regional traditions back to life. Monarchists such as Maurras, or Republicans did their utmost to revive Languedoc as a cultural entity. The same period also saw the birth of a "mystical spiritualism" created originally by the Romantic movement. Montségur was linked, by the end of the 19th Century, to the legend of the Holy Grail and the Cathar rock became the Montsalvat of Lohengrin and Parsifal, the myths recreated by Richard Wagner. Déodat Roché wanted to restore Catharism at the beginning of this century and he was not alone. There were those who talked of Esclarmonde of Foix or the Tibetan masters. "They see the troubadours and Knights Templar as hidden Cathars. They associate Catharism with Celtic Druidism, with the hyperborean solar cults of Thulé, with the Hindu tradition, with a Visigoth gnosis, or with pre-Roman cultures" (Jean-Louis Biget). The refusal to accept rationalism united all the followers of the occult, the esoteric and spiritism. They sought similarities between the myths, and principals which would unite all the religions. By participating in renewed unity, even if it was reserved for a small number of initiates,

-----

The Galamus gorge.

and the hermitage of Saint-Antoine.

they worked to find out more about the past and, in some cases, tried to divine the future. The nostalgic search for Catharism, though, suffered as a result of the works of Otto Rahn. He was a young German who assimilated the themes of the Neo-Cathars and, in 1933, published *Kreuzzug gegen den Graal (Crusade against the Holy Grail)*. The writer linked German traditions and the traditions of the troubadours of Occitania to prove that a tolerant, oecumenical pagan religion had united Europe under the symbol of the Holy Grail. He also stated that Cathar romanity and German tradition were similar inasmuch as the Visigoths had invaded, and settled in, what we now know as the South of France. In painful years such as these were, these ideas served the ideology of the German Nazis and Himmler recruited Otto Rahn for the Nazi propaganda bureau. After the war, however, Montségur could again be presented as the symbol of resistance to occupying forces. Fernand Niel saw Montségur as a solar temple, and he had plans to prove it. Pierre Benoît dreamed of Montsalvat, with its treasure trove and its fires. For, like the Knights Templar, the Cathars were said to have succeeded in saving their treasure before Montségur surrendered. And Klossowsi saw a reflection of Catharism in the works of the Marquis de Sade in which the good are the victims and the villains are triumphant. Television and novels helped to diversify views of Catharism. "Even so, the popularisation of knowledge, trade, anticlericalism or politics cannot explain everything. Indeed, they exploit the "imaginary world of the Cathars" more than they create it. Catharism contained some element that did not die out as the embers of the fires fell away to ash" (Jean Duvernoy).
Catharism, because it is shrouded in mystery, has encouraged intellectual metamorphoses, one might almost say off-shoots, such as poetic evocations and flights of fancy, theoretical constructions and magical practices, scholarly research and romantic reconstitutions. When History is silent, myth takes over. And myths are also an art form of the collective memory.

Since these men and women of days long gone have kept their secrets, we should keep silent about their unfortunate destiny. Yet legend would have it that the Cathars left a treasure somewhere. In fact, they did not hide away a hoard of precious metal; they concealed vague memories which are waiting to be rediscovered. Seen in this light, a historian's methods are more respectful of Catharism's painful past but, although prudence is wisdom and probity a safeguard, neither of them can eradicate history. On the contrary, they leave room for dreams.

Peyrepertuse.
The St. George Keep still has an observation window containing the lookout's seat.

opposite:
Puivert Castle looks as it is on fire as it stands out against the glow of the setting sun.

Places with Cathar Connections

Aguilar (Aude)

This castle stood guard over the entrance to the central Corbières region. It existed in 1021 and, in the 13th Century, belonged to the Lord of Termes. Then it became the property of the King of France. With Termes, Quéribus, Puilaurens and Peyrepertuse, this was one of the "five sons of Carcassonne". When these strongholds became the property of the King of France, they guarded the southern borders of his kingdom.
The 12th-century keep is encircled by an outer wall flanked by semi-circular towers. The tiny St. Anne's Chapel adds a religious note. It stands below the castle.

Aguilar Castle
which is known to have existed in the early years of the 12th Century.

below:
The East wall flanked by its towers.

Albi without the Albigensians. The heretics, who considered themselves quite simply as Christians and who referred to their Perfects as "Good Men", were often known as "Albigensians". Yet Albi was not a major centre of the Cathar faith (photo by Jeanne Duprat).

Albi (Tarn)

The heretics, who considered themselves as Christians and called their Perfects "Good Men", were often referred to as Albigensians and the crusade was launched "against the Albigensians". Yet, paradoxically, Albi was not one of the main centres of Catharism. It was because St. Bernard came to preach in Albi in 1145 and discovered the germs of heresy in this area that all the countries of Europe then began to refer to the Cathars of Southern France as Albigensians. The town was unaffected by the crusade; on the contrary, the bishop and population rallied to the support of Simon de Montfort. Yet the Cathar religion was not eradicated and there were some one hundred sentences passed on followers there between 1230 and 1330. A dozen or more Cathars were burnt at the stake. The admirable brick-built Cathedral of St. Cecilia on which building work began in 1277 was a symbol of the triumph of the Roman Catholic Church but its austerity also met the demands of the Cathars. The Bishop's Palace (La Berbie) now houses the Toulouse-Lautrec Museum.

Albi.

The organ in St. Cecilia's Cathedral (photo by Jeanne Duprat).

Alet-les-Bains (Aude)

This spa town with its wonderful climate was already known in the days of the Ancient Romans. Alet is a fine mediaeval town with a number of superb gates including the Porte Clavière, and a number of beautiful old houses including the Romanesque House. Its main historical importance, though, was its Benedictine Abbey, probably dating back to Carolingian times. It was in the second half of the 12th Century that it underwent major architectural alterations, as is obvious from the ruins left standing today. A huge church was built; all that remains of it now is its chevet, cloisters and a chapter house.

It was to this abbey that Bertrand de Saissac came to impose his will. He was the Viscount's regent until Raimond-Roger Trencavel came of age (1199) and, as such, enjoyed the confidence of these powerful noblemen. He was a well-known Cathar. When Abbot Pons Amiel of Alet died, the monks chose as his successor a man who did not find favour with Bertrand de Saissac. The warrior broke down the abbey doors, had the newly-elected abbot taken prisoner, and organised new elections. He had Pons Amiel's body exhumed, set it on the abbot's chair, and ordered the election of a new abbot who would be favourable to the Cathars. In doing so, this representative of a leading nobleman, himself a Cathar, reminded the monks, by violent means, that the lord enjoyed the right to control ecclesiastical power. Yet the same Bertrand de Saissac swore an oath to the Bishop of Béziers that he would not introduce Catharism into the viscount's lands.

In 1318, Alet became a bishopric and the minster became a cathedral. Bishop Guillaume d'Alzonne undertook to extend it by adding on a Gothic chancel and this building project lasted throughout much of the 14th Century. However, the Wars of Religion also left their mark on the region and the fine piece of architecture was destroyed and never recreated. The Bishops had to be content with the former monks' refectory as their place of worship. The most famous of all the bishops was the austere, highly-intelligent Nicolas Pavillon (1597-1677). He accepted this tiny diocese of only 30,000 souls and vigourously applied the Roman Catholic reforms, with all their attendant constraints. He was accused of jansenism and showed enormous obstinacy towards Louis XIV. Like the Bishop of Pamiers, he was one of the men who stood up against the royal will and, to do so, sought to obtain the backing of Rome.

Avignonet-Lauragais.
This statue of a crusader on a monument is a reminder of the soldiers who came from Northern France to take part in a crusade that had been launched by the Pope himself.

-----

opposite:
Arques.
The keep in Arques dates from a period after the crusade. It is a masterpiece of military architecture.

Avignonet-Lauragais (Haute-Garonne)

Heresy was rife in the Lauragais area and the Inquisitors were ruthless in their efforts to stamp it out. The Count of Toulouse had decided to launch another offensive against the King of France. His aim was to win the support of Cathar knights, even though he had participated personally in the repressive measures taken against the "heretics". He realised how unpopular the newly-created Inquisition was. "At the beginning of his campaign, he gave a totally unambiguous signal." The son of his half-sister (his father's natural daughter) was Raimond d'Alfaro who was in command of Avignonet. Raimond handed over the castle and Count's palace where the Inquisitors were billetted. Dispossessed lords (the *"faidits"*) then came down from Montségur under the leadership of Pierre-Roger de Mirepoix and were joined by other soldiers, making up a troop of some eighty men in all. As a matter of form, they pretended to break down the gates of the town on the night of 28th/29th May 1242 and murdered the two Inquisitors inside, a Dominican named Guillaume Arnaud and a Franciscan by the name of Etienne de Saint-Thibéry, along with their assistants. Ten men were assassinated that night. This was a premeditated act and other knights awaited the Inquisitors along the road in case they succeeded in escaping. They acted with the complicity of the townspeople, who left them to do as they wanted. Pierre-Roger de Mirepoix is said to have blamed one of his men for not bringing him back Guillaume Arnaud's skull so that he could use it as a drinking vessel. More importantly, though, the Inquisition's registers were destroyed; these registers were the result of meticulous enquiries on the part of the Inquisitors and formed the reason invoked for the use of torture. This assassination was a new threat on the part of the local population, the symbol of a renewed alliance between the Count of Toulouse and the heretics. Raimond VII was excommunicated but was finally forced to give in to the superior authority of Blanche of Castile and the King of France. Montségur, on the other hand, was a seat of resistance and, as such, left the monarch with no choice other than its destruction. There is a memorial called the Crusader of Avignonet. It is a reminder of the soldiers who came from the North of France in obedience to Church and Pope, to take part in a crusade to defend the Christian faith that was being threatened by a set of beliefs which was condemned by both i.e. the Albigensian heresy. The soldiers fought on this soil in the same way as other knights had fought in

Crusades against the Saracen in their efforts to reconquer the Holy Land. The idea of a crusade remained very much alive in the Western world until at least the 17th Century. The Albigensian Crusade, however, was not fought in distant lands; it set the knights against local populations. Like the wars between Catholics and Protestants in later centuries, the crusade was all the more terrible because it set brothers or cousins against each other.

Arques (Aude)

The village lies on the banks of the Rialsès. De Montfort entrusted Pierre de Voisins with the task of guarding this area of the Razès region after the Albigensian crusade. Gilles de Voisins commissioned the building of the castle in 1284. It was part of his plan for the defence of the Rialsès Valley and the roads leading to the Corbières or other, strongly Cathar areas. Historian Jean Duvernoy has shown that the Cathars also travelled along the paths used by farmers to take their livestock up to the summer alpine pastures. This meant that Arques and the Razès area, or Coustaussa and Cubières were linked to Prades, Montaillou and the Alion area. "Propaganda travelled along the same paths as sheep..." E. Le Roy Ladurie wrote, "In Arques, for example, now in the *département* of Aude, Sybille Pierre, a farmer's wife, knew all about the rumours rife in Montaillou. This was by no means surprising. The two villages, one in Ariège and the other in Aude, were twenty-four miles apart as the crow flies, but in fact they were adjacent communities since one was the centre of summer pasturage and the other a place in which livestock was wintered."
An outer wall encircles the castle. It includes a gate with machicolations topped by the Voisins coat-of-arms. The square keep with its four turrets dates from after the crusade and is a masterpiece of military architecture. It is 78 ft. high and has four storeys. The various rooms were built with outstanding care. This is a good example of progress in military constructions which were henceforth complex and skillfully-designed. They stood in a strategically-sensitive area. The village church was probably built by an-other member of the Voisins family at the end of the 14th Century. The stone-carving of the group of figures also dates from this period. Arques was the birthplace and final resting place of Déodat Roché. He was a magistrate and mayor of Arques, and he spent his entire life studying Catharism. It was he who started up the *Cahiers d'études cathares* and through his influence that the philosopher Simone Weil became interested in the Cathars. In 1940, she wrote a

now-famous letter on the subject, indicating that she considered Catharism to be a form of pythagorism or platonism with Christain overtones. Arques now has a Déodat Roché Museum.

Béziers (Hérault)

The army from the north headed for Béziers which the Viscount had fled, in order to fall back on Carcassonne. The Bishop of Béziers tried to convince the local population to surrender then he, in turn, left the town on 22nd July 1209. The town was captured and pillaged. The ransacking of Béziers is one of the major events in the crusade, even if the range of pillaging and the scope of the atrocities has been exaggerated. Arnaud Amaury is reported to have said, "Kill them all; the Lord will recognise His own!" This statement, reported by Césaire de Heisterbach, would seem to indicate that the crusade was changing. This was no longer a religious matter in which soldiers were undertaking police work in the name of the Church. This was no longer a traditional piece of feudal warfare limited in time and space. This was punishment for an entire population that had been considered as accomplices. For the barons of Southern France, it was a time of immense trial and tribulation during which their property lay under threat. For the ordinary people, it was an invasion during which everybody, even a good Roman Catholic, risked his or her life simply because family, friends or neighbours had chosen to follow the Cathars. Yet the army was too small.

During the Siege of Béziers, the attackers set fire to the Cathedral Church of St. Nazaire, built in the Romanesque era to designs by Master Gervais. At the end of the 13th Century, the nave was repaired. Thereafter, the cathedral continued to be embellished. The cloisters on the side of the cathedral date from the 14th Century. The Old Béziers Museum is now housed in the former Dominicans' Church. The Church of St. Mary Magdalen *(église de la Madeleine)* was at the centre of the massacre committed during the capture of Béziers in 1209. One version of the event tells how the local people had gone to the church and the priests had had the bells rung, as if for a funeral service. The foot-soldiers who assisted the knights and served as their valets, entered the town and began pillaging it. The French barons

Béziers.

A view over the cloisters from the bell-tower of St. Nazaire's Cathedral, with the countryside around in the distance (Photo by Pascal Moulin).

Carcassonne. The Count's Castle (in the background), west wall and Aude Gate.

wanted their share of the booty. The footsoldiers, annoyed by this, picked up torches and set fire to the town's buildings – the town was soon engulfed in flames. Mediaeval towns, built mainly of timber, were ideal targets for arsonists. The population in the church was said to have fallen victim to the fire that had spread throughout the town.

In the Church of St. Mary Magdalen, the transept and chancel are said to date from the 11th Century and the chancel from the 12th. This means that they survived the catastrophe. The Church of St. Aphrodise outside the town walls was a collegiate church with its own canons. The Trencavels made a generous contribution to its construction.

Bram (Aude)

This small town in the Lauragais area was a stronghold during the Middle Ages, with a high percentage of Cathars among its population. Simon de Montfort besieged the town and captured it three days later. In order to set an example, and because Cabaret (Lastours) was still resisting, he selected perhaps one hundred prisoners, had their eyes put out, and cut off their ears, noses and lips. Then he ordered one of the prisoners, who still had one eye left, to take his companions to Cabaret to strike fear into the hearts of the defending forces inside the fortress.

Bram is now unusual for its circular layout. The streets form concentric circles around the central church. This is characteristic of the hilltop towns or *"bastides"* built in South-West France in the 13th Century.

Carcassonne (Aude)

The young Viscount Trencavel was an ideal scapegoat during the Albigensian crusade. Béziers was pillaged and he surrendered Carcassonne. He was imprisoned and died shortly afterwards. His property was given to Simon de Montfort then to the King of France who annexed the town to the royal estates. The town is a summary of all that was best in the military architecture of the Middle Ages. The Trencavels had their castle on the west side. This late 12th-century fortress was built over a construction dating from the Dark Ages which had already replaced a Gallo-Roman building. The oldest section backs onto the western wall. The Count's Castle, though, was envelopped in fortifications built on the orders of the king once the town had surrendered. This was the work of St. Louis and Philip the Bold. In the 19th Century, architect Viollet-le-Duc completed the restoration of Carcassonne. The Count's castle was defended by six towers. It now houses a fine archaeological museum in which the most outstanding exhibits are a number of disk-shaped grave-stones often described, without any real proof, as "Cathar" stones. The round shape envelopped the Cross of Christ, concealing the symbol that the Manichaeans did not respect since they did not believe in God's reincarnation on Earth nor, consequently, in His death on Calvary.

The Inquisition Tower serves as a reminder of this fearsome ecclesiastical Court set up in the wake of the crusade. It developed rigourous methods of investigation to trace heretics in hiding. Those sentenced were imprisoned while the investigation continued. Their punishment was known as "The Wall".

During the Albigensian crusade, the outskirts of Carcassonne were razed to the ground because the population had rallied to the cause of their former lord, Trencavel, during his attack in 1240. A new town was therefore built, with a checkerboard layout, along the left bank of the R. Aude. It contained the parishes of St. Vincent's and St. Michael's

THE CATHEDRAL CHURCH OF ST. NAZAIRE IN CARCASSONNE

Building began on the Cathedral Church of St. Nazaire in the late 10th Century. The nave is Romanesque but the chancel and transept are Gothic. In the south arm of the transept is a slab said to mark the grave of Simon de Montfort, bearing the Cross of Languedoc and the de Montfort lion. A striking bas-relief shows an unidentified siege, but the so-called "siege stone" may depict the crusaders' attack on Carcassonne or Trencavel's attack in his efforts to recapture his town in 1240.

Near St. Anne's Portal in the Cathedral Church of St. Nazaire is a tombstone bearing the epitaph of Sans Morlane. He was one of the cathedral's almoners and, although not a Perfect himself, he is said to have attended Cathar meetings and his brother, Guillaume-Arnaud Morlane, Canon of Carcassonne, is said to have received the *consolamentum*. Sans Morlane was at the centre of a plot aimed at stealing the leather pouches in which the Inquisitors kept their files and the "evidence" proving the guilt of the heretics. The conspiracy was a failure. The Inquisitors continued their work and arrested a number of leading figures. Sans Morlane requested Pope Honorius IV to use his authority; the Pope had the file sent to him and declared it to be illegal. Sans Morlane died in 1311 without having been arrested and was buried in St. Nazaire's. Later, on the other hand, the bones of one of his cousins, Arnaud, were dug up and burnt.

named after the former suburbs. This is the "lower town" facing the walled town.
Pennautier Castle near the fortified town was de Montfort's headquarters during the crusade. The present castle was built in the 16th Century and altered in later years. It has superb grounds, laid out by Le Nôtre

Castelnaudary (Aude)

In 1211, after some of the crusaders had left, Simon de Montfort was besieged in Castelnaudary (said to be a weak town) by the Counts of Toulouse and Foix. However, they failed to take advantage of their superiority in numbers and a battle fought near the town remained indecisive. This shows the military superiority of de Montfort, one of the main features of the crusade.

Nearby is the **Mas-Saintes-Puelles**, doubtless named after two young girls who had been given the body of Saturnin, the saint-martyr. It was a major centre of Catharism and had a deacon and Perfects. The citadel was destroyed by Louis VIII during the crusade. **Molleville** Castle not far away is steeped in memories of Louis XVI's Minister for the Navy, Bertrand de Molleville.

Baraigne has a superb 15th-century castle with two round towers and one square tower. The courtyard is typical of the Renaissance style, showing that the castle was altered in the 16th Century or in later years, by the Buissons, the lords of this area. The church dates from the 12th Century. It contains a strange Sepulchre Cross decorated with an anchor, bird and triangular Cross. The graveyard has a number of disk-shaped stones.

The hilltop town of **Montferrand** still has its outer walls. It was once a citadel. The Count of Toulouse's brother, Baudoin, negotiated with Simon de Montfort and handed the town over to him.

From here, the **Naurouze** mountain pass is only a short hop away. This is the lowest, and shortest, crossing between the Atlantic and the Mediterranean. An obelisk was erected here in memory of Riquet, the admirable engineer who designed the Two Seas Canal. The local stones forming the base of the obelisk are cracked. Legend has it that, when the stones knit together again, the end of the world will be nigh.

Montmaur, literally "the Mountain of the Moors", was captured by de Montfort in 1211 and the Inquisition carried out investigations here. The fortified castle in the centre of the village was built in the 15th Century. Four round towers flanked the awesome construction, although it has lost some of its austerity thanks to the addition of mullioned windows. The keep stands in the centre of the castle. The Church of St. Baudile dates from the 15th Century and disk-shaped gravestones stand beside its chevet.

Saint-Paulet still has its 13th-century castle, which was altered during the Renaissance and the 17th Century. This was the property of the La Tour d'Auvergne family, one of whose sons was the famous Maréchal de Turenne, Louis XIV's great general. His heart has been buried here since 1819. Again, the graveyard contains a number of disk-shaped stones.

Saint-Papoul was initially a Benedictine abbey, founded in memory of the apostle from the Lauragais area. In 1317, it became a bishopric, one of the tiny bishoprics that lasted until the French Revolution. The cathedral includes a 12th-century chancel but the nave dates from a later period, as do the cloisters.

left:
Castelnaudary, the law courts.
The King of France made his presence felt through his justice system. This building was the home of a seneschal before becoming the seat of a «*présidial*», or court of law, in the 16th century.

above:
The Naurouze Threshold.
An obelisk has been erected in memory of Riquet, the engineer who designed the Two Seas Canal.

right:
Montmaur.
A disk-shaped stone beside the chevet of St. Baudile's Church.

Coustaussa (Aude)

The fortress in Coustaussa was built in 1157. It was initially occupied, without a fight, by de Montfort but later, in 1211, he was obliged to lay siege to it. Despite this, the area remained loyal to the Cathars. At the beginning of the 14th Century, there were still a number of Perfects who came from Coustaussa. The castle now lies in ruins.

Cucugnan (Aude)

This village was made famous by one of Alphonse Daudet's tales, which would seem to suggest that Cucugnan was in Provence rather than in Languedoc! In the story, the good priest dangled visions of Hell before the eyes of his parishioners in order to encourage them to lead more pious lives. Cucugnan lies in the very heart of Cathar country, near Peyrepertuse and Quéribus.

Durban-Corbières (Aude)

Durban lies in the heart of the Corbières. All that remains of the castle high above the village is a superb façade with 16th-century windows. Visitors setting off on the trail of the Cathars should not forget that this is also a major wine-producing area.

Durfort (Aude)

This citadel was built on a spur of rock flanked on all sides by the Orbieu and the natural beauty spot became a lookout post, standing guard over the gorge leading to Termes. The castle is known to have existed in 1093.

The family that owned these lands was influential and strongly attracted to Catharism. However, the castle was captured by the crusaders in 1215. Ramparts and corner towers are still standing but most of the castle lies in ruins. The main apartments date from the 17th and 18th Centuries.

Fanjeaux (Aude)

It is difficult to imagine, as you stroll through the quiet streets of Fanjeaux, that this was once a town with numerous noblemen, and a major centre of Catharism; it even had a number of houses belonging to Perfects. St. Dominic wanted to meet the aspirations of Cathars in order to encourage them to return to the Roman Catholic Church. He therefore settled in Fanjeaux and spent nine years there trying to rid the Lauragais area of the heresy. It was here that he saw God's sign, a comet, which led him to set up a community in Prouille where converted women Perfects could lead the same life as they had before, without breaking off their connections with Rome. A memorial to this Seignadou has been erected; from it, there is a panoramic view of the Lauragais Plain.

St. Dominic's house occupies the former castle tack-room; the castle no longer exists. The saint's bedroom has become an oratory.

St. Dominic's Chapel in the parish church contains the beam that bears witness to the miracle of the fire. The sheet of paper on which Dominic had written during the Montréal debate was not destroyed by the flames; instead, it flew up to the roof and left scorch marks on a beam! The chancel was richly decorated in the 18th Century. There is a Cross set into the parapet of the bridge. It is a Cross of Toulouse but historians no longer consider that these strange Crosses have any connection with Catharism.

Foix (Ariège)

The Counts of Foix protected the Cathars and the women of this illustrious family were themselves Perfects. Raimond-Roger of Foix is said to have attended the ceremony at which his sister, Esclarmonde of Foix, was made a Perfect, even though he remained loyal to the Roman Catholic faith. His wife, Philippa of Foix, had no doubt also been attracted by the Cathar faith; she retired to Dun. Simon de Montfort launched a number of attacks on Foix without ever succeeding in capturing the castle. Yet he had boasted, or so says tradition, of "being able to melt the rock of Foix like grease over a flame" and "to roast the master on it". In 1215, Raimond-Roger handed over the fortress, which was returned to him in 1218. In 1229, his son, Roger-Bernard, submitted to royal authority and the Counts remained powerful noblemen until the end of the Middle Ages.

The Count's Castle has two square towers dating from the early 13th Century, as proven by a seal. The round tower was built at the beginning of the 15th Century. The castle was spared despite Richelieu's determination to dismantle all fortresses. It was used as a prison.

Fanjeaux.
The village in which St. Dominic lived
while preaching against the Cathar religion.

Foix. The Counts Castle.
Despite his best efforts, Simon de Montfort was unable to capture it.

Fontfroide (Aude)

The monks set up communities in lonely spots and Fontfroide lies well off the beaten track. The Order of Cîteaux gave new impetus to the old Benedictine Order that had previously ruled the lives of the men of God. It was the Cistercians who fought against the heresy discovered by their spiritual leader, St. Bernard, in the South of France.
However, the Cistercians did not succeed in stamping out the advance of the Cathar faith. They seemed to live too well in their fine rural abbeys. The Albigensians, on the other hand, made a virtue of poverty and renunciation. For many years, the Roman Catholic Church tried to negotiate with the heretics, even while they were busy condemning the heresy itself. Pierre de Castelnau, a monk from Fontfroide Abbey, was a papal legate who accused the Count of Toulouse of complicity. His murder led directly to the Albigensian crusade. Jacques Fournier was born in the 1280's in the North of the county of Foix and was doubtless of modest extraction but one of his uncles was already Abbot of Fontfroide. After studying at Paris University, he succeeded his uncle and became Abbot of Fontfroide in his turn. He was famous for his scholarliness and was chosen as Bishop of Pamiers where he was noted for his determination to root out heretics and by his "obsessive, excessive, but competent investigations" (E. Le Roy Ladurie). Later, he became Bishop of Mirepoix. The Inquisition Register he drew up in Pamiers has been studied on several occasions and formed the basis of historian E. LeRoy Ladurie's work, *Montaillou, an Occitan Village*. In 1327, Jacques Fournier was made a cardinal; in 1334, he became Pope in Avignon under the name of Benedict XII. He was an austere monk who sought to introduce greater morality into the monasteries and impose his rigourous views of dogma.

Lagrasse (Aude)

The Corbières region was wild and untamed, an area that was to attract the men of God who, from the Middle Ages onwards, sought solitude in order to be able to pray. As always, the monks attracted an entire population and a town was built near the monastery. The powerful Lagrasse Abbey was founded in the 8th Century by Nimphridius, a friend of St. Benedict of Aniane. A mediaeval novel, *Philomena*, probably written in praise of the abbey, tells how Charlemagne himself was its founder. During his campaigns against the Saracen, Charlemagne is said to have discovered hermits who had taken a vow of silence and ate nothing but bread. One of them is said to have worked the miracles of the five loaves. This story shows the extent to which the monastic community was capable of imagining its own history in order to exalt its background and increase its power. Relations were often strained between Lagrasse Abbey and the local noblemen, especially the Lord of Termes. The Abbot backed de Montfort in his crusade while the Lords of Termes supported the Cathars. The abbey enjoyed its heyday under Abbot Auger (1280-1311). Like other abbeys, Lagrasse enjoyed a new lease of life after accepting the St. Maur Reform in 1663.
The town, set opposite the abbey, has retained its mediaeval charm. It still has sections of town wall, including the 12th-century Plaisance Tower, some beautiful old houses and the covered market decorated with coats-of-arms. The Old Bridge (12th Century) spans the R. Orbieu. The main features of the abbey are its abbot's apartments with cloisters on the ground floor, a guardroom on the first floor (15th Century) and, in the abbot's chapel (late 13th Century), frescoes representing the Last Judgement and the Rod of Jesse. The 13th-14th century monks' dorter is a vast chamber with ribbed arching.
The bell-tower/keep was built on the hillside in 1537. Other abbey buildings were constructed in the 18th Century, giving this abbey (like many others) a more worldly, castle-

Lagrasse.
The small town of Lagrasse has retained its mediaeval charm, with the remains of its town walls and a number of splendid old houses.

THE CLOISTERS OF FONTFROIDE

Although the austere, huge church in Fontfroide dates from the 12th Century, its magnificent cloisters, in which the galleries have ogival vaulting, were built in the 13th Century, at the time the Established Church was engaged in eradicating the heresy. The cloisters open onto the chapter house where the monks' council (the Chapter) held its meetings. Four marble colonnettes support nine ogival vaults. The dorter has a superb 12th-century vaulted roof. The monastery was given additional embellishments in the 18th Century.

like appearance. It had a main courtyard, cloisters and a fine staircase.

Nearby is the Pre-Romanesque Church of **Saint-Martin-des-Puits** which contains frescoes dating from the first half of the 12th Century.

Lastours (Aude)

The first known reference to Cabaret dates from 1063. Thereafter, the Lords of Lastours acknowledged the sovereign rights of the Viscounts of Béziers and Carcassonne. They were also on excellent terms with the monks in Fontfroide. Yet at the end of the 12th Century, the Lords of Cabaret began to protect the Cathars and a community of Perfects was set up here.

The outlines of the four castles in Lastours, set in the same spot in the heart of the Cabaret area, serve as a reminder of the pride of feudal lords but, at the same time, as an indication of the gradual loss of their power and influence and the fragmentation of their system of defence. From north to south, the castles are Cabaret, Tour Régine, Surdespine and Quertinheux. Cabaret was the dominant castle and it had control over the surrounding area along the edge of the Montagne Noire. Pierre-Roger de Cabaret was one of Trencavel's companions; he was also one of the Trencavels' vassals. His whole life was marked by the Cathar faith that he protected, perhaps without actually being a Cathar himself.

The crusaders' first attack on Cabaret failed and Bouchard de Marly, a relative of Simon de Montfort, was taken prisoner. He was a valuable negotiating tool in 1211 when Pierre-Roger de Cabaret was forced to capitulate. He was compensated for the loss of his castles. Despite his submission, the Lords of Cabaret remained hostile to the Catholic crusade and, in 1223, they regained ownership of their lands. A Cathar Bishop, Pierre Isarn, stayed in Cabaret c. 1223, preaching to the local nobility. He was burnt at the stake in 1226. Another siege occurred in 1227. It was a failure but the women Perfects had to be evacuated. In the end, the citadels fell. By 1243, the four castles of Cabaret had become royal fortresses. Yet Catharism remained alive for many years and the

-----

Lastours.

Cabaret is the largest of the castle and it gave its name to one of the phases in the Albigensian conflict; the others are Tour Régine, Surdespine and Quertinheux.

castellans of Cabaret received the *consolamentum*, despite the fact that they had been appointed by the King of France himelf. This proves that, at the end of the 13th Century, the entire general staff of Cabaret remained true to the Cathar faith. The strategic importance of these castles explains why they were altered and refurbished so often. The alterations were aimed mainly at adapting them to progress in artillery and cannons.

Cabaret is the most heavily-fortified of them all. It consists of a keep with an ogival-vaulted chamber on the first floor, apartments, and an outer wall.

The village of Salsigne nearby is famous for its mines, in particular for the gold mine that was worked from 1892 onwards. Cabrespine Castle was captured by Simon de Montfort's troops.

Les Cassès (Aude)

There were large numbers of Cathars in this area, which depended on the Lords of Saint-Félix. During the crusade, knights from Toulouse surrendered here and handed the castle over to the crusaders, with the Perfects who had sought refuge in it. The bishops entered in order to convert them. It was a thankless task. The crusaders took hold of them and sent "some sixty of them, with immense joy" to the stake (G. de Puylaurens).

The old graveyard used to contain disk-shaped stones which, for many years and no doubt wrongfully, were thought to be of Cathar origin or inspiration. A strange statue also aroused a great deal of comment. On one side are three disks set out to form a triangle; on the other is a bearded figure. However, the figure (who is, of course, Christ) is not really Christ Crucified. Instead, he is said to be stretching out His arms in prayer rather than suffering on the Cross. He is said to have His feet on the ground, i.e. He is alive. René Nelli considered this to be "one of the few figurative remains of the Cathar faith and perhaps the only work of art to have been directly influenced by Bogomilism". This would indeed seem to indicate a refusal of God's sacrifice and, therefore, of His incarnation.

Lastours

Views of Tour Régine and, in the background, Quertinheux castle.

Lordat (Ariège)

The castle used to stand high above Ariège, keeping guard on the Sabarthès area. Yet this region was deeply marked by the Cathar heresy and the marks were to remain for many years. This was a major location in the County of Foix and the castle existed here in the 11th Century. The Counts of Foix were quick to follow the Cathar faith. The citadel was not threatened by the crusaders but it was used as a refuge by the Cathars. The Lords of Lordat were Cathars and there used to be a Cathar graveyard here. Help was sent out to Montségur from here. The castle still has its keep and the remains of its three outer walls.

Miglos (Ariège)

The local nobleman was a Cathar and the isolated, ruined castle, shows the destiny of families such as this one, attracted to a new faith and struck down in its name.

Nearby are the **Niaux Caves**, where the paintings have been compared to the ones in Lascaux.

The Vicdessos Valley had a number of iron mines. This led to the setting up of the so-called Catalonian ironworks.

The castle in **Montréal-de-Sos** was once a fortress belonging to the Count of Foix. All that now remains of this 13th-century fortress are a few stretches of wall. It seems that the system of defence included the caves round about. According to one report, the four "heretics" who had succeeded in fleeing Montségur during the siege found refuge in this castle. A cave painting found below the castle depicting a drinking vessel, a sword, and drops of blood led to a Pyrenean version of the legend of the Holy Grail. According to mediaeval legend, the Holy Grail was the cup into which Christ's blood flowed when the centurion pushed his lance into His side. Chrétien de Troyes was the first person to write about the quest for the Holy Grail and, in the late 19th Century, Richard Wagner used the theme again in his operas. An abundance of literature sprang up stating that the Holy Grail had been brought to the Pyrenees. In fact, there was confusion between two different legends, one referring to the Holy Grail and the other concerning the Cathars' treasure trove. Otto Rahn exploited this theme in his Crusade against the Holy Grail. Later, he would appear to have worked for the Nazis' propaganda department. The aim was to evoke an original, magical form of Christianity which is said to have been handed down to the Cathars because the Roman Catholic Church had moved away from its origins as a result of Jewish influence and had begun to persecute the true Aryans. The Nazis even tried to file the names of wizards, witches or heretics who had been sentenced centuries before by the ecclesiatical authorities; they considered these people to be their mythical ancestors!

Minerve (Hérault)

Minerve, in the heart of the area that bears its name, lies in the foothills of the Cévennes in a landscape carved out by two rivers, the Cesse and the Brian. Roman, and later Visigoth, settlements show that man lived here many years ago in large numbers as seen in St. Nazaire's Church where the white marble altar dates from 456 A.D. and bears the name of St. Rustique, Bishop of Narbonne.

At the time of the crusades, only the castles of Termes and Cabaret were mightier than the fortress in Minerve, according to one of the chroniclers of these dramatic times. The mediaeval town provided a refuge for Cathars after the ransacking of Béziers. The name of one of the Perfects who died has been handed down to us today – Guillaume de Cadre. The people of Narbonne complained about the raids carried out by the people of Minerve. Simon de Montfort decided to besiege the town in 1210. Some 700 men and their followers set off then spread out around the town. They had a catapult, perhaps the one known as "La Malevoisine". The town's water supply came from a well at the foot of the cliff, reached by a fortified staircase. Guillaume, Lord of Minerve, capitulated on 22nd July 1210 after a siege lasting

left:

Minerve.

A memorial to those who died at the stake.

One hundred and forty Cathars refused to abjure their faith and were burnt at the stake.

-----

below:

Mirepoix.

The tomb of Constance of Foix, wife of Jean de Lévis.

seven weeks. Arnaud Amaury laid down the conditions of the capitulation. The besieged population was allowed to go free, along with any Cathars who would agree to submit to the will of the Established Church. The crusaders entered the town and 140 Cathars preferred to die at the stake rather than abjure. Only three women Perfects were saved, thanks to the intervention of the mother of one of the crusaders. This was the first time in the crusade that Cathars had been burnt at the stake. A garrison was then billetted in the town. Guillaume de Minerve, after submitting for a time, continued to fight the noblemen from the North. His son took part in the Trencavel revolt in 1240 but later rallied to St. Louis' cause and accompanied him on a crusade to the Holy Land. In 1258, the King of Aragon handed over all his rights in the Minerve area and it became French. The monarchy set up its own administration here, initially with a bailiff then with a mere provost. The town was much-prized again during the Wars of Religion and Louis XIII finally ordered the demolition of the fortifications in 1636.

Minerve still has its old-fashioned charm with its gates, the covered path leading to the well, and two outer walls. The Church of St. Stephen *(église Saint-Étienne)* has an 11th-century chancel and a 12th-centry nave; it has all the austere beauty of Romanesque architecture. All that remains of the castle is the candela (a tall, slender tower) and one wall to the east overlooking the Brian Gorge, but these sections date mainly from the days of the royal fortress built after the end of the crusade.

Mirepoix (Ariège)

The town used to be part of the County of Foix. In 1207, the Count granted the population a charter. Catharism, though, was becoming increasingly widespread in the town and several Perfects' houses (perhaps 50 in all) had been set up there. In 1206, a council brought some 600 Cathars together. They may have discussed doctrine or they may have decided to strengthen the defences of a number of castles, such as Montségur. As to the Mirepoix family, it had a number of great defenders of the Cathar cause. In 1209, de Montfort captured Mirepoix and entrusted it to his lieutenant, Lévis. Pierre-Roger de Mirepoix tried to retake his town but died during the siege. In 1221, again in Mirepoix, there was a meeting between dignitaries of the Cathar church and members of the local nobility, no doubt aimed at providing protection for the persecuted. In 1229, however, Gui de Lévis

became Marshal of Mirepoix, with a brief to guard the entire area. The second Pierre-Roger de Mirepoix was one of the defenders of Montségur; he was a cousin of Raimond de Péreille to whom the fortress belonged.
In 1279, the Puivert dam burst and the town of Mirepoix was carried away by the flood water. The local people asked their lord to rebuild the town in a more secure location. Jean de Lévis then had this hilltop town designed with a regular layout. The main square is typical of the hilltop towns, or *"bastides"*, with its row of timbered houses forming galleries that provide protection against the sun or bad weather. On the Consuls' House, the beams were decorated with carvings of human heads or monsters. In 1317, Mirepoix became a bishopric and the Church of St. Maurice became a cathedral. Should these new bishoprics, among them Saint-Papoul, Alet and Pamiers, be seen as a determination on the part of the Roman Catholic Church to gain a stronger grip on an area where Catharism had made a very definite mark?
Lagarde Castle not far away is representative of the new powers of the de Lévis who obtained from Simon de Montfort the citadel that had once belonged to the Counts of Foix. The fortress was built by Gui III de Lévis in the 14th Century and altered during a later period.
The village of Camon is said to have been founded by Charlemagne. It is more probably a village that originally grew up around a monastery, known in French as a *"sauveté"*.

Montaillou (Ariège)

Only a few ruins of the castle are still standing. This village owes its recent fame to a book written by historian Emmanuel Le Roy Ladurie in which he studied, in an unusual manner, the registers drawn up by the Inquisition while preparing to pass sentence on the local population who had remained loyal to the Cathar faith.

Lagarde.
The ruins of the castle built by Gui III de Lévis in the 14th Century.

Camon.
This tiny village in Ariège still has extensive traces of its erstwhile fortifications.

Montréal (Aude)

A debate was held in Montréal in 1207. The Roman Catholic Church was represented by Diego, Dominic, Pierre de Castelnau and his colleague, Raoul; the Cathars included Arnaud Hot, Benoît de Termes, Pons Jourda and Guilhabert de Castres. The chronicler of the event recounted how each of the sides remitted their writings to arbitrators, in this instance two noblemen and two wealthy merchants. The discussion is said to have lasted a fortnight. The remainder of the story is shrouded in legend. "One of our men, named Dominic, a man steeped in saintliness who had been the companion of the Bishop of Osma, wrote down the quotations that he had used during the debate. He gave the piece of paper to one of the heretics so that he could review the man's objections. During the night, the heretics gathered round the fire in a house. The one to whom the man of God had given the sheet of paper handed it round his companions. They then suggested that the paper should be thrown into the fire. If the paper burned, their beliefs (i.e. their misbeliefs) would be proved to be true. If, on the other hand, it did not burn, they would confess the truth of the credo put forward by our preachers." The paper withstood the flames three times. However, the theological debate held in Montréal, even if it did not lead to any obvious results, was a victory for the Cathar Church which was able to discuss matters with the representatives of the official Church on an equal footing. Diego of Osma left Languedoc but his follower, Dominic, remained behind.
All that remains of the Middle Ages is a huge Gothic collegiate church (St. Vincent's, 14th Century with later alterations). The nearby L'Espérou stands on the site once occupied by the castle.

Montségur (Ariège)

The spur of limestone rock in the part of the Pyrenees lying within Ariège, which rises to a height of 3,923 ft. and is topped by Montségur Castle, is commonly known as a "pog".
It was Raimond de Péreille who agreed to build fortifications on this spot in the early 13th Century and it is difficult to know what stood on the peak before this date. The Cathars made it their refuge as the crusaders and the Catholic Church multiplied their offensives.
The driving force behind this resistance was Guilhabert de Castres. He was the man who had welcomed Esclarmonde of Foix into the Cathar Church and it was he who had attended

the debate at Montréal. He sought refuge in Montségur and turned to the nobility of Catalonia for assistance. In 1221, he met two of the great feudal lords of the Pyrenees in Mirepoix, for this very purpose. Taking advantage of the lull in hostilities, he began to preach openly in the lowlands, but the renewed offensive by the royal army forced him to flee. After the Count of Toulouse' submission in 1229, a large group led by Guilhabert de Castres begged Raimond de Péreille to give them shelter in his citadel at Montségur where the heretic church would thenceforth have its "seat and its head". There, Guilhabert proceeded with ordinations. From there he sent out his deacons and Perfects and it was there, too, that he defended them.
Knights settled in Montségur with their equerries, living off the treasure trove belonging to the Cathar Church. The treasure was amassed thanks to believers who made bequests when they were on their death beds or who asked their heirs to do so on their behalf. The money was also used to pay barons who agreed to protect the Perfects in return for payment.
The royal army wanted revenge for the attack on the Inquisition. Montségur was the key to the resistance to the king and the Church and, as such, had to be captured. The garrison consisted of some three hundred and forty people, led by Pierre-Roger de Mirepoix and Raimond de Péreille, his first cousin and father-in-law. There were 160 lay people including 27 women and 20 sergeants, and 180 Perfects. Guilhabert de Castres was dead; he had been succeeded by Bertrand Marty. It is difficult to imagine what the castle looked like at that time, for it has doubtless been altered since then. However, Montségur was a difficult place to supply with food and water. The siege began in the spring of 1243. It was led by Seneschal Hugues des Arcis of Carcassonne, accompanied by Pierre Amiel, the Archbishop of Narbonne, and the Bishop of Albi. Because of the lie of the land, it was impossible to cut the fortress off – a number of audacious men managed to slip into the castle regularly to take in news from outside. Eventually, it was Gascons who climbed the mountain at night and succeeded in capturing a look-out post. The Bishop of Albi, a skilful engineer of heavy weaponry, set up a catapult which sent stones raining down on the people inside the castle. Another engineer, Bertrand de Capdenac, succeeded in entering Montségur. However, on 1st March 1244, Pierre-Roger de Mirepoix surrendered. He had negotiated the surrender and requested that the lay people be allowed to go free, but he handed over the Perfects who had to choose between abjuring their faith and being burnt at the stake. Almost two hundred of them died in the flames. "The fall of Montségur was a symbol. Yet even though it marked the disappearance of the most consummate "monastery" complete with hierarchy, a "Mother Superior" of the women Perfects, houses and monthly "services", it did little to change the preaching habits of the many "clergy" still operating underground" (Jean Duvernoy). A disk-shaped memorial was inaugurated on 6th June 1960 by the *Société du souvenir et des études cathares* in memory of the events that took place in the "Field of Those Burned at the Stake".
The keep at the very top of the pog was encircled by an outer wall. A village huddled between the castle and the edge of the breathtaking cliffs. To the south, the castle was protected by a succession of walls – visitors, then as now, arrived from this direction. To the north-east, a lookout tower stood on the Roc de la Tour. This was the rock captured by the Gascons, thereby posing a threat to the castle's occupants during the siege.
Four Cathars managed to escape. They may have been asked to save sacred books or keep safe a treasure. It is said that two Perfects had already evacuated the treasure in 1243. Thereafter, imagination took hold of the episode. Based on the writings of Wolfram von Eschenbach, a German troubadour, Montségur was assimilated to the castle in the legend of the Holy Grail and the idea was taken up again in the 20th Century by Otto Rahn who seems to have then worked for Himmler and the Nazi propaganda department. However, given that the Cathars showed great disdain for the material things in life which were manifestations of Evil, it seems highly unlikely that they would have placed much value on magical relics.
The de Lévis family took possession of the castle. In 1924, the Duke de Lévis-Mirepoix wrote a book on Montségur.
The fortress was altered at the end of the 13th Century or at the beginning of the 14th and the remains that visitors see today date from this period although a few features of the older citadel survived. This has enabled archaeologists to

-----

Montségur: the "pog".

It was Raimond de Péreille who agreed to build fortifications on this spot in the early 13th Century and it is difficult to know what stood on the peak before this date. The Cathars made it their refuge as the crusaders and the Catholic Church multiplied their offensives.

contest the theories that Montségur was a Cathar temple or even a place used by sun-worshippers.

After the rebuilding, the keep was integrated into the system of defence and was no longer in the centre of the castle. On the first floor, there were probably the main apartments; they were reached from the parapet walkway. The lower section of the keep consisted of a water tank and a low-roofed chamber. It was flanked by a building followed by a poultry yard. An artificial moat separated this fortified building from the barbican to the East.

Archaeological digs remained secret in Montségur for a long time. They were linked to the rediscovery of Catharism but then became more controlled and more scientific. They have revealed numerous objects that were part of everyday life in Montségur during the Middle Ages but none of them enlightens us about Catharism.

Even if historians and archaeologists succeed in resisting the wildest flights of imagination, Montségur impresses everybody for the beauty of its setting and for the memories of a drama that can leave nobody unmoved since it was the paradoxical combat of two fundamental values of humanity – faith and liberty.

Narbonne (Aude)

Narbonne has been a harbour and a prosperous town since the days of the Roman Occupation and, in the 12th Century, it was governed by Viscountess Ermengarde who held a "Court of Love" in her palace at which she encouraged poetic creativity. More particularly, though, the Bishops of Narbonne were immensely influential throughout the South of France and the Archbishops', or Old, Palace dating from the 12th Century is a fine illustration of this power. The Archbishop of Narbonne soon rallied to the crusaders' cause against the Albigensians. Arnaud-Amaury, Abbot of Cîteaux, who was in charge of the crusade, became archbishop here in 1212, which shows that this see was of major importance. Archbishop Gilles Aycelin had the keep of the new palace built at a later date. The Gothic cathedral was not built until 1272.

Narbonne, the cathedral.

Even if the Bishops of Narbonne had a leading role in Languedoc area and even if one of these prelates became a pope called Clément IV, they didn't succeed in forcing the completion of this sanctuary, which was then a simple choir, on the town middle-class (photo by Pascal Moulin).

Padern (Aude)

This castle used to belong the Lagrasse Abbey. It was occupied during the crusade then recaptured by its dispossessed lords or *"faidits"*, warriors who refused to accept the domination of the crusaders or the King of France and who preferred to live like outlaws. The castle then stood watch over the Franco-Spanish border. With Peyrepertuse, Quéribus and Aguilar, this constituted an admirable line of defence. The fortress underwent extensive alterations thereafter in order to improve its defences but the work was pointless since the borders were redesigned and were further away from the castle.

Pamiers (Ariège)

A meeting took place in Pamiers in 1207, attended by Diego of Osma, St. Dominic's master. The Count of Foix' Court seemed the ideal setting for a meeting between Catholics and Waldenses (they were followers of Pierre Valdo and were often regarded as heretics but they hesitated to acknowledge any connection with Catharism). In Pamiers, there were bishops and abbots on one side and Waldensian clerks on the other headed by Durand de Huesca. Arnaud de Crampagna had been chosen as arbitrator. The most important point of this meeting was that Esclarmonde of Foix, who was in fact a Perfect, wanted to take part in the debate. She was prevented from doing so by a monk in these terms, "Get back to your distaff, woman! You have no place in a debate of this nature." This ticking-off showed that women had been an important influence in the spread of the heresy, especially as literature had praised their role through the concept of courtly love. It also showed that the reaction demanded by the Church was beginning to make itself felt and that women were to return to their place as subordinates traditionally bound to total obedience. The meeting was definitely effective. The arbitrator found against the Waldenses and they, in turn, rallied to the orthodox views of the Established Church and were pardoned. Durand de Huesca even wrote a number of texts condemning the heretics.

In **Vals** on the Mirepoix road, there is a cave-church decorated with 12th-century frescoes of Byzantine inspiration.

Mazères is a *"bastide"* (hilltop town) with a regular urban layout built on land belonging to the nearby Boulbonne Abbey. This was the birthplace of Gaston de Foix, Duke of Nemours and hero of the Battle of Ravenna in 1512 where he lost his life.

Padern, the sentinel.

This castle used to keep watch over the marches of Spain.
With Peyrepertuse, Quéribus and Aguilar, it provided an admirable line of defence. The fortress has been altered in more recent times to turn it into a comfortable residence.

Pamiers.

A close-up of the bell-tower on the cathedral
(photo by Jean-Pierre Siréjol).

IMPREGNABLE PEYREPERTUSE

Its setting and geographical location brought Peyrepertuse the reputation of being impregnable and the line of rocky hills known as the Upper Corbières kept watch for many years over the border between the kingdoms of France and Aragon, until the Treaty of the Pyrenees was signed in 1659. Until then, the castle had been one of the "sons of Carcassonne" with Aguilar, Termes, Quéribus and Puilaurens. Peyrepertuse, though, enjoyed relative peace. It may be that a Queen of Castile, Blanche, the neglected wife of Peter the Cruel and cousin of the King of France, lived here. What is certain is that Henry of Trastamara, Peter's rival, took refuge here after defeat in Navarette in 1367 and that Du Guesclin, Constable of France, was imprisoned here. In 1369, Henry became King of Castile.

Since the fortress was seldom subject to attack, it is permissible to wonder whether the King of France ordered its reinforcement to improve its defences or to make a symbolic show of strength in the direction of Aragon. The length of the outer walls (one-and-a-half miles) and the quality of their construction makes this the most outstanding piece of mediaeval architecture in Languedoc. It is often referred to as the "Celestial Carcassonne".

Peyrepertuse (Aude)

It was during Charlemagne's reign that the Peyrepertuse area was first mentioned. Its name, Petra Pertusa, may mean "pierced rock". The castle is mentioned in the will of Bernard Taillefer, Count of Besalu, son of one of the Counts of Barcelona who died in 1020.

Gradually, the Peyrepertuse and Fenouillède areas were integrated into a powerful Spanish kingdom on the borders of the kingdom of France. Peyrepertuse constituted the northernmost limits of this Spanish kingdom. And marriages were used to rebuild what inheritances, in an area without any real right of succession for the eldest son, sometimes broke up.

A Peyrepertuse family appeared and seemed to be linked to the fate of the Viscounts of Narbonne. However, Peyrepertuse was apparently spared by the crusaders from the north in the early years of the 13th Century and, in 1217, Guilhem de Peyrepertuse paid homage to Simon de Montfort, who had become Duke of Narbonne. However, Guilhem later took up the fight again against the French crusaders and captured Puilaurens. He was then excommunicated.

Even in those days, the destiny of this area was dependent on international politics and the regent of the Kingdom of Aragon sold Peyrepertuse Castle to King Louis IX of France. The French then had to capture it. The citadel played a part in the vast campaign led against Trencavel in 1240 but the war was lost and, in November 1240, Guilhem de Peyrepertuse submitted to his new master, whose chamberlain, Jean de Beaumont, pursued Trencavel's army as it retreated. Peyrepertuse was thereafter one of the castles standing guard over the south-ern borders of the kingdom of France, as confirmed in the Treaty of Corbeil signed in 1258.

The nearby village of **Duilhac-sous-Peyrepertuse** stands on a hilltop. St. Michael's Church dates from the 12th Century but its belltower is 19th Century. It stands on the highest point, the Fort, which was, therefore, protected. The village grew up around the church during the Middle Ages.

Peyrepertuse.

In the Middle Ages, the art of fortification consisted first and foremost of using the defences provided by Mother Nature. An army could not leave a citadel in the rear; it had to be captured. Yet a fortress like Peyrepertuse seems to be impregnable.

PUILAURENS: STONE LOOKOUTS

Although the keep was built prior to the Albigensian Crusade, most of the fortress was built during the reigns of St. Louis and his son, Philip the Bold. This area was the setting for countless battles between the French and the Spaniards. In 1473 and 1495, Puilaurens was besieged, but in vain. The system of defence was completed at the end of the 16th Century and in the 17th. Not until 1635 and the beginning of the great Franco-Spanish War did Puilaurens fall to 800 Spaniards. When the Treaty of the Pyrenees was signed, the border was redesigned, further south.

The entrance to the citadel stands up the hill, at the top of a right-angled flight of steps. The fortress itself consists of two outer walls, the first of which enclosed a large, elongated courtyard. The north wall follows the lie of the land, effectively extending and reinforcing the spot's natural defences. The jagged crenelations can still be clearly seen. A postern gate to the south-east, protected by the tower, leads onto the platform high above the surrounding countryside. A second wall encircles the small area around the "keep".

Only this square tower had been built by the time of the crusade, probably in the 12th Century. Entrance was by way of a gate defended by a machicolation. High above the path is the so-called White Lady Tower (perhaps in memory of Blanche of Bourbon who is said to have stayed here when travelling south to marry Peter of Castile). Between its two storeys, it has a duct through the wall that acts as a speaking tube.

Views of Puilaurens.

Prouille (Aude)

St. Dominic founded a religious community in Prouille in 1206 for Cathar women whom he had brought back into the Catholic fold. It was natural, and therefore easier, to slip from Albigensian purity to Dominican renunciation. In 1879, a new convent was built to replace the one that had been destroyed during the French Revolution. Prouille is a centre of Dominican spirituality. A pilgrimage is held here early in October every year, to honour the rosary given to St. Dominic by the Blessed Virgin Mary.

Puilaurens (Aude)

Puylaurens or, to be more exact Puylaurent as it used to be written, became Puilaurens in order to differentiate it from Puylaurens-du-Tarn. Puilaurens stood watch over the Boulzane and Upper Aude Valleys. The castle is referred to in 985 A.D. in a papal bull issued by John XV. At that time, it belonged to the great Abbey of Saint-Michel-de-Cuxa.

The first castellan of Puilaurens still known today was Pierre Catala who was Guillaume de Peyrepertuse' witness when he submitted to Simon de Montfort. Guillaume, however, took up the fight again and was excommunicated by the Archbishop of Narbonne who launched a campaign against him. Guillaume was then the commander-in-chief in Puilaurens. Roger Catala appears to have been the owner of the castle at that time and he suffered yet again during the struggle against the King of France i.e. when Trencavel returned in 1240 and the Count of Toulouse rebelled in 1242. Cathars are known to have been present in Puilaurens in the 1240's. In 1246, a deacon came from the Cabaret area at the foot of the Montagne Noire and settled in Puilaurens before moving on to become deacon of the Fenouillet area in Quéribus. The fortresses, though, fell one after the other into the hands of the King of France and his seneschals. After the fall of Montségur, Puilaurens finally became a French possession, probably before 1250, but Chabert de Barbeira may have prolonged the resistance here, as he did in Quéribus. In 1255, St. Louis ordered the Seneschal of Carcassonne to add fortifications to Puilaurens Castle.

The castle was built mainly after the area had surrendered to the King of France, for him and by him. Puilaurens was, thereafter, one of the "sons of Carcassonne", designed to stand guard over the border.

Nearby is the Upper Aude Valley and the spectacular **Pierre-Lys** Gorge. The present road was built in the 18th Century, with the backing of the local priest. Not far away is the peak known as **Bugarach**, the highest mountain in the Corbières.

Puivert (Aude)

Puivert stands high above the Kercorb, or Chalabre, area. In 1170, a meeting of troubadours was held here and Peire d'Auvergne recorded the events in one of his poems. He said that he composed it, "to the sound of the bagpipes in Puivert, among songs and laughter". The meeting was held after a princely marriage, that of Alphonse VIII of Castile and Eleanor, daughter of Henry II Plantagenet and Eleanor of Aquitaine. With the 12th Century, courtly literature became increasingly common and human love became the main theme, perhaps at the expense of divine love.

When the crusade was launched, the castle belonged to Bernard de Congost. His wife received the *consolamentum* on her deathbed from Perfects, and Bernard died in Montségur. Their daughter, Saissa de Congost, became a Perfect and was one of those burnt at the stake in Montségur on 16th March 1244.

Pons de Bruyères, one of de Montfort's companions, came to the Kercorb area and captured Puivert. Later, the Bruyère family obtained the title to Puivert. It was then that a strange natural disaster occurred. There was a lake at Puivert at that time. Work, perhaps commissioned by Jean de Bruyères, caused the catastrophe in 1279. A dam, thought to have consisted of boulders, gave way and water from the lake swept through the valley, destroying the town of Mirepoix further downstream. Had the Lord of Bruyères wanted to lower the water level in order to extend his land? Or, as the fine legend has it, did he want to please a princess from Aragon who had retired to Puivert? She enjoyed resting on a rock on the edge of the lake but complained of the waves whipped up by the wind. Jean de Bruyères'gallantry did the rest – and both rock and princess were swept away by the water. A real troubadour's tale! One of the Lords of Bruyères was Chamberlain to Philip the Bold and accompanied him to war. This brought tax advantages for the area.

The Bruyères decided to embellish the castle and most of the buildings date from the first half of the 14th Century. The keep consists of three chambers, one above the other. There is a guardroom, a chamber with ogival vaulting and the so-called musicians' chamber. The second chamber was probably a chapel. A niche known as the "fountain" was possibly the piscina used in Christian liturgy. The room was lit by two large windows. The vaulting is decorated with a carving representing the Virgin Mary and a figure of St. Michael slaying the dragon. The brackets are decorated with figures carrying phylacters, and scrolls bearing inscriptions. Despite historic tragedy, Puivert has retained a long-standing love of music. The brackets also have eight carvings representing musicians and their instruments i.e. bagpipes, a viol (the forerunner of the violin), a small drum, a lute, a portable organ, a triangular psaltery and a rebeck (forerunner of the violin). Throughout history, Puivert has had a number of lords and, in 1680, it became a marquisate. Before the French Revolution, the castle belonged to the Roux family.

In Puivert village, the Kercorb Museum has memorabilia relating to the area and the castle.

Not far away is **Chalabre**, the main town in the Kercorb area. It lies at the confluence of three valleys (Hers, Blau and Mirepoix) and was the scene of bloody fighting between crusaders and local people. The traditional "charivari" (street revelry beneath the windows of older men who marry young girls) has been maintained. It is held on 12th December.

Puylaurens-du-Tarn (Tarn)

This castle was a refuge for Cathars. Before the crusade, Sicart de Puylaurens had attended the funeral of a knight named Peytavi de Puylaurens in the Cathar graveyard. He had agreed to accommodate Guilhabert de Castres in his citadel in 1223 and a Cathar doctor in 1226. These were public commitments to the Cathar faith. The crusade, however, changed the course of events. The French met with strong resistance. Puylaurens was doubtless occupied for some time by French noblemen,

-----

Puivert (top and middle).

– A bracket in the chamber on the second floor of the keep. Eight carvings depict musicians and their instruments i.e. bagpipes, a viol, a small drum, a lute, a portable organ, a triangular psaltery and a rebeck (a forerunner of the violin).

– The East wall containing the entrance.

Prouille: St. Dominic's wager (bottom).

In 1206, Dominic had a vision of a comet in Fanjeaux and Le Seignabou serves as a reminder of this event. Dominic set up a community in Prouille for Cathar women whom he had converted and it was easier for them to slip from the purity of their Albigensian lifestyle to the renunciation of the Dominican Order. The present convent dates from the return of the Order of St. Dominic to this spot in the 19th Century.

since Raimond VII of Toulouse had them decapitated in punishment for the rape and atrocities that they had committed. Finally, Sicart de Puylaurens paid homage to the King of France in return for his lands. A man named Guillaume de Puylaurens also wrote a Chronicle. The ruins of the 13th-century castle conjure up images of this painful history.

Not far away is **Saint-Paul-Cap de Joux** (Tarn), one of the resting-places used by St. Bernard when he undertook the extensive travels through the South of France that made him realise how widespread the Cathar heresy had become. The town was also the usual place of residence of Cathar Bishop Gaucelm although he travelled to Toulouse, where he died c. 1225-1228. Guilhabert de Castres was another visitor to the village.

Quéribus (Aude)

For many years, the danger came from the sea and numerous citadels were built, like Saracen towers, keeping watch over the horizon. Then the fortresses became an integral part of a political context built up by marriages and bequests around Barcelona, Aragon and Provence. Quéribus was one of the strongholds that defended the northern marches of this vast domain.

It is difficult to imagine a more daring citadel, or a more amazing look-out post. Quéribus is also steeped in memories of one of the most outstanding figures in the resistance shown by the people of Southern France, Chabert de Barbeira. He had extensive knowledge of fortifications and he was commander of Quéribus. The citadel defied Rome and the king and it served as a refuge for Cathars such as Benoît

Quéribus, looking towards the Mediterranean.

Three outer walls protect the huge keep which was, from the very outset, the main element in the system of defence. In the first walls, the loop-holes show that the citadel had been adapted to take account of developments in artillery fire. The second wall protected a chamber that must have been used as a barracks room by the soldiers. The keep is polygonal in form and flanked by a rectangular tower. Its most outstanding feature is the superb Gothic room known as the Pillar Chamber. "The majesty of this place is summarised in the might of the pillar exploding into a sort of palm tree with irregular branches forming the vaulted roof" (M. and J.-B. Gau). A recess opens onto a stone-mullioned window. There was doubtless an earlier keep (a few traces of it are still visible today) but most of the building work was carried out in the second half of the 13th Century as a result of royal determination to reinforce and strengthen these border castles. The stair-case tower was added at that time.

de Termes, Bishop of the Razès area, who died there in 1231. Chabert de Barbeira was given military command of the strongholds in the Fenouillet area that were still independent, when the King of France's troops arrived in 1242. But, in 1239, the regent of the kingdom of Aragon had sold Quéribus to King Louis IX. All that remained for the French monarch was to conquer it. In the end, in 1255, Chabert was obliged to surrender and he handed Quéribus over to St. Louis. This meant that Quéribus actually resisted longer than Montségur. The conditions under which the stronghold was surrendered remain unclear. It was said to be Olivier de Termes, the former companion of the Cathars who had, in the meantime, become close to the King, who captured Chabert in an ambush. Chabert's life was spared. Royal, i.e. French, authority predominated. The castellan who then settled in Quéribus was appointed by the Seneschal of Carcassonne. Although Quéribus had put up fierce resistance to the crusaders, troops from Aragon captured it in the 15th Century without any difficulty, but the stronghold was later retaken by the French.

Quérigut (Ariège)

The castle lies in the Donnezan area. It used to belong to Bernard d'Alion who accommodated Perfects on his land. He was pursued by the Inquisition and burnt at the stake. He had married Esclarmonde of Foix, who was a Perfect, and he was therefore the Count of Foix' brother-in-law.

Rennes le Château (Aude)

Redae had been the Visigoth capital of the Razès area and a large town in the Early Middle Ages but it was pillaged and destroyed in 1170 by the King of Aragon and never regained its former importance. Rennes-le-Château, a hilltop village set further north on a spur of rock, was the successor to this past. It was there, in 1885, that a new parish priest arrived. His name was Bérenger Saunière. He is said to have discovered a treasure in his church which enabled him to restore the sanctuary and erect a number of buildings such as the Villa Béthanie or the Magdala library-tower. Was it a Gallic or Visigoth treasure trove or did it come from the Cathars? The same Father Saunière is also said to have discovered a number of mysterious manuscripts and to have gained access to circles with an ardent love of esoterics, perhaps even political circles. He is even said to have aroused the interest of the Hapsburgs! What is certain is that he altered his church and included a number of surprises such as Asmodel the Devil supporting the stoup. The strange parish priest was condemned by his bishop and no explanation was ever found for his luxurious lifestyle. Rennes-le-Château still attracts people in search of mystery.

The surrounding area includes the following:

Blanchefort is a Visigoth fortress that may have been destroyed during the Albigensian crusade.

The castle in **Couiza** belonged to the Voisins who were granted ownership by de Montfort. In the 16th Century, it passed into the hands of the Joyeuse family who built a new castle on the site (1540-1562). The outside of the house is still mediaeval in appearance but inside is a fine court-yard built in the Renaissance style.

Rennes-les-Bains has existed since Roman times. It was they who built baths here to take advantage of the hot spring waters and their numerous properties. Blanche of Castile stayed here and this may explain the town's current name, a transformation of "bains de la Reine" or "Queen's Bath".

Roquefixade (Ariège)

This castle existed in the 11th Century. It was strengthened in 1270, during the reign of Philip the Bold, when the King of France fortified the border to the south of his kingdom. Like many other citadels, Roquefixade kept watch over roads, in this case the road linking Foix and Mirepoix, and it was this function that gave these fortresses their political and strategic importance.

left, top:
The castle of Quérigut.

Saint-Félix-Lauragais is said to have hosted a Council of the Cathar Church in 1167. The meeting was chaired by a "pope" from Constantinople.

Roquefixade.
Like many citadels, Roquefixade was designed to keep watch over roads, in this instance the one from Foix to Mirepoix. It was this role which gave these fortresses their political and strategic importance.

Rennes-le-Château.
Asmodel the Devil supporting the stoup.

Saint-Félix-Lauragais (Haute-Garonne)

A Pope or "papas" is said to have come from the Cathar church in Constantinople in 1167 to chair a council held in Saint-Félix de Caraman (now known as Saint-Félix de Lauragais). A document, which is the subject of some controversy, tells how bishops were chosen for Lombardy, Northern France, Albi, Toulouse, Carcassonne and Agen and how limits were suggested for a Cathar church that was beginning to look like a counter-Church, with its own hierarchy. The largest number of bishops was said to have been appointed for Languedoc, a sign perhaps that the heresy had found more fertile ground and a higher number of followers there than elsewhere. The town still has some fine mediaeval buildings including a 14th-century church, a covered market and some superb houses. The castle dates from the 12th and 13th Centuries.

Saint-Gilles (Gard)

It was Saint-Gilles that formed the basis of the Count of Toulouse' power. Raimond, Abbot of Saint-Gilles-du-Gard, the Count's younger son, had gained power and influence in the 11th Century and had gathered under his control land stretching from Provence to Gascony.

It was in Saint-Gilles that the papal legate, Pierre de Castelnau, was murdered in 1208. This event led to the breaking off of relations between the Count of Toulouse and the Pope who then launched the crusade. The legate was buried in the crypt of the church. In 1209, Count Raimond VI made penitence before the door of the church in Saint-Gilles and was whipped by the papal envoy.

The church still has its beautiful 12th-century West Front, a masterpiece of Romanesque architecture. It shows the extent of the power wielded by the Benedictine abbey.

Saissac (Aude)

Saissac stands on the slopes of the Montagne Noire, the southernmost end of the Massif Central. This was a centre of Catharism very early on in the history of the heresy. Bertrand de Saissac, regent until Raimond-Roger Trencavel came of age, protected the Cathars. The castle was captured from his lords by Simon de Montfort who gave it to his companion-in-arms, Bouchart de Marly.

Saissac.

This village has some fine old houses.

It was a centre of Catharism in the very early days.

This estate, which depended on the Counts of Carcassonne, was given to the de Lévis in the 13th Century.
The village, which has some fine old houses such as the Saptes Residence, was built on the banks of the R. Vernassonne. Two crenelated towers serve as reminders of the fact that this was a walled town in the 12th Century. One of the towers now houses a museum.
Downhill from the village, rather than uphill as is more usual, is a castle, built on a spur of rock surrounded on all sides by sheer cliffs. This fortress dates from before the crusade. All that remains of the original castle is the keep with its huge walls and a few underground chambers. The castle was initially dismantled then extended in the 16th Century.
St. Michael's Church, between castle and village, is of Romanesque origin but it underwent alteration in the Gothic and Classical periods.
Montolieu, a town in the vicinity, is said to get its name from the fact that it marked the limit at which olive trees would grow. A royal linen factory in the suburbs made this a prosperous town in the 18th Century. The fortifications were destroyed by St. Louis' men after Trencavel had been defeated.

Villelongue Abbey is Cistercian. It was built in the 13th Century but went into a decline and is now part of a farm. One of the galleries in the cloisters still exists and has columns with carved capitals. All the features typical of Cistercian buildings can still be seen i.e. the chapter house, dorter on the first floor, refectory, calefactory, undercroft and lay brothers' dorter. The size of the church ruins are an indication of the past power of the abbey.

Termes (Aude)

The castle was first mentioned in 1110. It stood in a border area and was a fearsome fortress with a reputation for being impregnable. It was well protected by deep precipices gouged out by the R. Sou, a tributary of the Orbieu. The family who owned Termes were vassals of the Viscounts of Carcassonne-Béziers, who were themselves vassals of the Counts of Barcelona. Members of the family dominated the entire Termes region.
The Termes family was deeply involved in the Cathar adventure. Raymond de Termes held the castle in the village of the same name. His brother, Benoît de Termes, was appointed Cathar Bishop of the Razès area in 1226. This meant that a heretical hierarchy was apparently opposed to the Roman

Catholic Church. Benoît took part in the Cathar council in Pieusse which was chaired by Guilhabert de Castres, Cathar Bishop of Toulouse.

Simon de Montfort besieged the castle in Termes in 1210, in one of the crucial turning-points of the Albigensian crusade. "Our valiant and cunning enemies, as soon as our machines broke through a section of wall, immediately built another wall behind it with stones and timber..." This account by Pierre des Vaux de Cernay is an excellent description of the resistance put up by the noblemen of Southern France when faced with the army of crusaders. All that was known of the art of building fortifications was used to provide support for the heretics. The citadel was able to resist for four months but the main problem was the water supply. The town was about to surrender when rain filled the water tanks again but the water was polluted and the besieged population fled the town. However, Raymond de Termes was captured and died in prison. His sons, Olivier and Bernard, were brought up at the Court in Aragon. The castle was given to one of de Montfort's companions-in-arms, Alain de Roucy. Olivier de Termes took up the battle again but was finally obliged to bow to royal authority. He decided to accompany Louis IX on a crusade to the Holy Land and set sail from Aigues-Mortes in 1248. Louis IX's prestige as a devout Christian and respected monarch made it easier for noblemen to rally to his cause in this way. Olivier de Termes returned to the Holy Land several times and the chronicler, Joinville, paid homage to his courage. He took part in the capture of Quéribus and the defeat of his ex-companion-in-arms, Chabert de Barbeira.

The castle in Termes became a royal possession and the king kept a garrison there. According to a document dated 1483, this was one of the five "sons of Carcassonne" set along the borders of France. The others were Puilaurens, Aguilar, Quéribus, and Peyrepertuse. The citadel came into its own again during the One Hundred Years' War and even during the Fronde Revolt against the young Louis XIV. In 1652, it was decided to demolish it, especially as it was, by then, far from the Spanish border and, therefore, much less useful that it had been.

The castle used to consist of two concentric rings of walls which have suffered badly from the passage of time. Most of the work doubtless followed the crusade, when the monarchy wanted to strengthen its new acquisitions.

A rectangular building in which the vaulting has collapsed may have been a 12th-century chapel. Note the fine Cross-shaped window. The parish church in the village dates from 1163.

opposite:

Termes.

– A former flue in the castle.

– A buttress at the north-west corner of the castle. At the top, there used to be a bartizan but it has now disappeared.

-----

attached:

Muret.

The memorial commemorating the terrible battle that took place here on 13th September 1213.

Toulouse (Haute-Garonne)

Toulouse was at the very centre of the Albigensian crusade for the end-purpose of the crusade was to weaken the independence of the Count of Toulouse vis-à-vis the Church and the King of France. He was to be prevented from acquiring support, yet again, from a new ecclesiastical hierarchy. The King of France wanted to put an end to the principalities that were limiting his own sovereignty.

Toulouse was the cradle of the Order founded by St. Dominic in order to combat heresy. The Black Friars received from the Pope himself the task of reconquering souls by words and by persuasion. Pierre Seila and one of the first Dominican friars donated several houses in Toulouse. Dominic lived there.

The Dominican Church in Toulouse (*église des Jacobins* – the Order was also named "jacobins" after its friary in the Rue Saint-Jacques in Paris) shows their determination to provide austerity, rigour and grandeur as a framework for their preaching.

Near Toulouse, only half-a-mile from Muret, a terrible battle was fought on 13th September 1213. It resulted in the death of the King of Aragon and victory for the crusaders despite the fact that they had been outnumbered. There is a memorial to this event.

Ussat-les-Bains (Ariège)

In the vicinity of Ussat, a spa town specialising in the treatment of nervous disorders to which Lamartine was a frequent visitor, there are countless fortified caves with real or mythical connections to the story of Catharism. The caves are known as "spoulga". They were fortified by local noblemen so that they could be integrated into systems of defence and were doubtless used by persecuted Cathars. According to Jean Duvernoy, it was Antonin Gadal who was instrumental in bringing about the popularity of such tales. "A. Gadal, the man responsible for taking visitors through the caves in Ussat was well-acquainted with the legends and details provided by his profession and he invented them when none such existed. This being so, the young "Wandervogel" Otto Rahn was to find all the information he needed for his Crusade against the Holy Grail which crystallised all the brief and long-worn details of musicology and archaeology that surrounded the myth" (Jean Duvernoy). According to René Nelli, A. Gadal was, on the contrary, "one of the patriarchs of modern Catharism". His collections were reproduced by the Rosicrucians in Holland, an indication of the links between all these movements based on hermetism and esoterics and the interest that a number of contemporary groups such as Rosicrucians or Freemasons have in beliefs of a bygone age e.g. Catharism. Ussat is even said to be a particularly privileged spot. "It is also said by occultists to be subject to extremely beneficial telluric radiations and, if they are to be believed, corresponds to one of the "preserved" areas in the Western world" (René Nelli).

The caves at Bethléem include a rock drawing of a pentagon, said to be a favourite symbol with Cathars and to have been used in initiation rites. The person being initiated was said to stand in the pentagon with arms and legs apart. "This pentagon is part-natural and partly painted by the hand of man and must date from protohistoric times. Yet it is probable that the Cathars noticed it in the 13th Century and treated it with a degree of veneration. Among the geometrical symbols most commonly reproduced by them is the pentagon set within a star with five branches and formed, one might say, by this very star" (René Nelli). A dove engraved on copper said to be of Cathar origin is reported to have been found by A. Gadal. The cave in Lombrives belongs to the same subterranean network as the cave in Niaux but, unlike the latter, has no cave paintings. Nature, on the other hand, has carved out some wonderful shapes to which man has given evocative names such as The Petrified Waterfall, the Mammoth or Pyrene's Tomb. There are also strange legends surrounding the cave. It is said that Cathars were walled up alive in it. During his visit to Ussat, Henri IV who was a descendent of

THE DOMINICANS' CHURCH IN TOULOUSE

The Dominican Church in Toulouse: speech as the way to conquest.

Toulouse was the cradle of the Order founded by St. Dominic. The Preaching Friars were ordered by the Pope himself to reconquer people's souls by the power and persuasiveness of their preaching. This Gothic church had the honour of being chosen as the final resting place of St. Thomas Aquinas (photo by Pascal Moulin).

the Counts of Foix, had the cave opened again and discovered the remains of the unfortunate Cathars. He then had them given a Christian burial. This shows a determination to see in the Cathars forerunners of the Protestants, since Henri IV was a Protestant for many years until he was converted to the Roman Catholic faith.
The cave, or spoulga, in Bouan on the road from Ussat to Ax-les-Thermes, looks like a castle clinging onto a rock. The North cave still has its door and crenelations.

Usson (Ariège)

The Alion family tried to escape the storm clouds that were gathering. It had numerous possessions, especially in the Donnezan area with Ussan and Quérigut. The Lords of Alion claimed the title of Viscount. Bernard d'Alion and his brother, Arnaud d'Usson, joined the crusaders then, in 1226, Bernard d'Alion paid homage to Louis VIII of France. However, he married Esclarmonde, the sister of Roger-Bernard II of Foix. She was to become a Perfect and she carried with her the Cathar inheritance of her house. The witnesses at the wedding were all believers and dispossessed noblemen *("faidits")*. This took the family into the troubled 1240's. Bernard d'Alion and his brother tried to provide assistance for Montségur in 1244 by sending a Catalan brigand chief into the fortress with 25 sergeants. Usson provided shelter for the Perfects and the treasure taken out of Montségur may have been brought here. It is thought that the four people who escaped Montségur travelled through here.
Bernard d'Alion was burnt at the stake in Perpignan in 1258 in the presence of James of Aragon. "He was the victim of a vast operation carried out against the Cathar nobility in the Fenouillet area by the King of Aragon at a time when, under the terms of the Treaty of Corbeil, he was about to hand the area over the King of France" (Jean Duvernoy). The Inquisitor in Languedoc had helped the Inquisitor in Aragon in return for assistance for those besieged within Montségur.
The castle was rebuilt in the 13th Century and altered when Louis XIV gave the fortress to the Marquis of Usson. Sold off as national property during the French Revolution, it was then used as a source of building stone. Its keep, though, has retained its proud appearance.

Verfeil (Haute-Garonne)

The chronicler, Guillaume de Puylaurens, has left a colourful account of St. Bernard de Clairvaux' trip to Verfeil in 1145. The fearsome abbot had become aware of the rapid strides being made by heretical beliefs in the South of France and he wanted to bring people back into the fold of the Established Church. In his sermon, he attacked the nobility which had let itself be attracted by Cathar ideas. There were large numbers of noblemen and, as estates were divided up each time they passed from one generation to another, there were one hundred or more co-lords in Verfeil alone. The noblemen left the church, followed by the ordinary people. Bernard then followed them into the street, continuing to preach at them. They covered the sound of his voice by banging on all the doors so Bernard, using a figure of speech that was particularly popular in the Middle Ages (the pun) shouted "Verfeil (Verte Feuille or "green leaf"), may God wither you!" Verfeil was thereafter considered as the "Seat of Satan" or the "Synagogue of Satan".

-----

left:

Usson.

The castle was rebuilt in the 13th Century but underwent extensive alterations when Louis XIV gave it to the Marquis d'Usson.

below:

The fortress in Villerouge-Termenès

was probably built during the second half of the 13th Century.

Villerouge-Termenès (Aude)

This castle belonged to the Archbishop of Narbonne, which shows that the prelates integrated well into feudal society and that ecclesiastical power was based on grand estates. The Archbishops, though, had to defend their property against their neighbours both before and after the Albigensian crusade.

Villerouge lay in the heart of a vast estate, for the Archbishop owned a large number of villages in the locality and received tithes or taxes. In order to ensure that these dues were paid to him and that his vassals were governed correctly, he used a bailiff and Villerouge lay in the middle of the bailiwick.

The Archbishops of Narbonne did their best to fortify the castle and its size and sheer mass are impressive. The large tower, or keep, at the south-east corner includes three rooms one above the other, each with very thick walls in which staircases were built. There is a crenelated terrace.

The citadel was probably built in the 13th Century during the third quarter of the century perhaps. Was this a sign of renewed determination on the part of the ecclesiastical authorities to provide better defence for their property and, consequently, a will to preserve it more efficiently?

It was in the castle in Villerouge-Termenès that Guillaume Bélibaste, said to be the last surviving Perfect, was burnt at the stake. He had been born nearby in Cubières in 1280. He led a nomadic life after killing a shepherd who wanted to denounce him to the bailiff on the grounds that he was a Cathar. He was initiated by Philippe d'Alairac and became a Perfect. He was arrested but escaped from Carcassonne then lived in Catalonia. Perhaps in order to conceal his true identity, he lived with a woman, which was contrary to the rules imposed on Perfects. He returned to France to provide support for the Cathars and was denounced by one of them to the Inquisition. He died in Villerouge-Termenès on 24th August 1321. The life of this last Perfect is the subject of a number of historical works.

Bibliography

History

La Chanson de la croisade albigeoise, adaptation by Henri Gougaud, introduction by Michel Zinc, preface by Georges Duby, Paris, 1989.

DOSSAT (YVES), *Les Crises de l'inquisition toulousaine au XIIIe siècle (1233-1273)*, Bordeaux, 1959.

DUVERNOY (JEAN), *L'Histoire des cathares, La Religion des Cathares*, Toulouse, 1976 ; *Le Catharisme*, Toulouse, 1979.

DUVERNOY (JEAN), NIEL (FERNAND), NELLI (RENÉ), ROCHÉ (DÉODAT), *Les Cathares*, Paris, undated.

GUIRAUD (JEAN), *Histoire de l'Inquisition au Moyen Âge*, Paris.

LE ROY LADURIE (EMMANUEL), *Montaillou, village occitan*, Paris, 1975, 2nd. edition 1982.

MUSY (JEAN), « Mouvements populaires et hérésies au XIe siècle en France », *Revue historique*, No. 513, January -March 1975.

NELLI (RENÉ), *La Vie quotidienne des cathares du Languedoc au XIIIe siècle*, Paris, 1969.

NELLI (RENÉ), *Les Cathares*, Paris, 1972.

NIEL (FERNAND), *Albigeois et Cathares*, Paris, 1955.

RAPP (FRANCIS), *L'Église et la Vie religieuse en Occident à la fin du Moyen Âge*, Paris, 1971.

ROQUEBERT (MICHEL), *L'Épopée cathare* ; vol. 1, *L'Invasion* ; vol. 2, *Muret et la Dépossession* ; vol. 3, *Le Lys et la Croix* ; vol. 4, *Mourir à Montségur*, Toulouse, 1971-1989.

ROQUEBERT (MICHEL) ET SOULA (CHRISTIAN), *Citadelles du vertige*, Toulouse, 1966, 2nd. edition 1990.

SCHMIDT (CLAUDE), *Histoire de la secte des cathares ou albigeois*, Paris-Genève, 1849.

SIVERY (GÉRARD), *Blanche de Castille*, Paris, 1990.

THOUZELLIER (CHRISTINE), *Catharisme et Valdéisme en Languedoc à la fin du XIIe et au début du XIIIe siècle*, Paris, 1966.

TESTAS (GUY ET JEAN), *L'Inquisition*, Paris, 1966.

WOLFF (PHILIPPE), *Histoire de Toulouse*, Toulouse, 1958.

Among the admirable series of *Cahiers de Fanjeaux* created by MARIE-HUMBER VICAIRE, we used the following:

> *Saint Dominique en Languedoc*, 1966.
> *Cathares en Languedoc*, 1968, réédition 1989.
> *Paix de Dieu et Guerre sainte en Languedoc au XIIIe siècle*, 1969.
> *Historiographie du catharisme*, 1979.
> *Bernard Giu et son monde*, 1981.

Archaeology

A few of the outstanding monographs published by the *Centre d'archéologie médiévale du Languedoc*:

BAYOU (LUCIEN), *Le Château de Puylaurens*, 1981.

BAYOU (LUCIEN), *Le Château de Villerouge-Termenès*, 1988.

BAYOU (LUCIEN), *Le Château de Termes*, 1988.

BURJADE (MADELEINE ET FRANÇOISE), BAYOU (LUCIEN), *Le Château de Peyrepertuse*, 1983.

GARDEL (MARIE-ÉLISE), *Les Châteaux de Lastours*, 1981.

GAU (MICHEL ET BERNARD), *Le Château de Quéribus*, 1983.

SARRET (JEAN-PIERRE), *Le Château de Montségur*, 1985.

SARRET (JEAN-PIERRE), *La Cité de Minerve*, 1985.

TISSEYRE (JEAN), *Le Château de Puivert*, 1982.

The minster in **Fontfroide** dates from the 12th Century; its cloisters, with their ogival vaulting, from the 13th.

Places with a Cathar Connection

Albi (Tarn)
Alet-les-Bains (Aude)
Avignonet-Lauragais (Haute-Garonne)
Arques (Aude)
Béziers (Hérault)
Bram (Aude)
Carcassonne (Aude)
Castelnaudary (Aude)
Coustaussa (Aude)
Cucugnan (Aude)
Durban-Corbières (Aude)
Durfort (Aude)
Fanjeaux (Aude)
Foix (Ariège)
Fontfroide (Aude)
Lagrasse (Aude)
Lastours (Aude)
Les Cassès (Aude)
Lordat (Ariège)
Miglos (Ariège)
Minerve (Hérault)
Mirepoix (Ariège)
Montaillou (Ariège)
Montréal (Aude)
Montségur (Ariège)
Padern (Aude)
Narbonne (Aude)
Pamiers (Ariège)
Peyrepertuse (Aude)
Prouille (Aude)
Puilaurens (Aude)
Puivert (Aude)
Puylaurens-du-Tarn (Tarn)
Quéribus (Aude)
Quérigut (Ariège)
Rennes-le-Château (Aude)
Roquefixade (Ariège)
Saint-Félix-Lauragais (Haute-Garonne)
Saint-Gilles-du-Gard (Gard)
Saissac (Aude)
Termes (Aude)
Toulouse (Haute-Garonne)
Ussat-les-Bains (Ariège)
Usson (Ariège)
Verfeil (Haute-Garonne)
Villerouge-Termenès (Aude)

Map: Patrick Mérienne.

-----

opposite:

Puilaurens.

The "Weavers' Cross"

in Mas-Cabardès (Aude). The heretics were sometimes referred to as "Weavers".

Table of contents